The Ultimate Collection of Cultural Artifacts
A Chronicle of Humankind's Greatest Achievements

PUBLISHED BY Julian Cross

J. Cross

© Copyright 2024 - All rights reserved.

All introductions, analyses, and commentaries contained within this book may not be reproduced, duplicated, or transmitted without direct written permission from the author or the publisher. Under no circumstances will any blame or legal responsibility be held against the publisher or author for any damages, reparation, or monetary loss due to the information contained within this book, either directly or indirectly.

Legal Notice:

This book is only for personal use. You cannot amend, distribute, sell, use, quote, or paraphrase any part of the introductions, analyses, or commentaries within this book, without the consent of the author or publisher.

Disclaimer Notice:

Please note the information contained within this document is for educational and entertainment purposes only. All efforts have been executed to present accurate, up-to-date, reliable, complete information. No warranties of any kind are declared or implied. Readers acknowledge that the author is not engaged in the rendering of legal, financial, medical, or professional advice. The content within this book has been derived from various sources. Please consult a licensed professional before attempting any techniques outlined in this book.

By reading this document, the reader agrees that under no circumstances is the author responsible for any losses, direct or indirect, that are incurred as a result of the use of the information contained within this document, including, but not limited to, errors, omissions, or inaccuracies.

The Ultimate Collection of Cultural Artifacts

Table of contents

Introduction 5

Chapter 1: Echoes from Antiquity 9
1.1 Ancient Innovations that Shaped Civilization 9
1.2 Artifacts of Faith and Belief 13
1.3 Wonders Lost and Found 16
1.4 Tools of Survival and Daily Life 19
1.5 Currency and Trade Artifacts 23

Chapter 2: Masterpieces in Stone and Marble 29
2.1 Expressions of Empire and Glory 29
2.2 Temples of the Spirit 30
2.3 Stone Megaliths and Mysteries 33
2.4 Spaces of Civic Life and Public Identity 35

Chapter 3: Canvas and Colors – Revolution in Art 41
3.1 Artistic Movements that Changed Perception 41
3.2 Iconic Masterpieces and Their Secrets 44
3.3 Artifacts as Cultural Commentary 46
3.4 Portable Masterpieces and Everyday Aesthetics 48

Chapter 4: Literature's Timeless Voices 53
4.1 Books That Shaped Humanity's Conscience 53
4.2 Literary Milestones of Cultural Exchange 55
4.3 Writers Who Challenged Conventions 57

Chapter 5: The Symphony of Humanity 60
5.1 Instruments that Transformed Music 60
5.2 Musical Works Defining Eras 63
5.3 The Cultural Impact of Rhythm 65

Chapter 6: Science's Game-Changers 68
6.1 Groundbreaking Discoveries 68
6.2 Inventions that Altered the Course of History 72

6.3 Science as a Cultural Catalyst 74

6.4 Scientific Instruments and Devices 76

Chapter 7: Engineering Wonders and Human Ingenuity 81

7.1 Structures that Defied Limits 81

7.2 Innovations in Transport and Mobility 85

7.3 Infrastructure as Cultural Landmarks 88

7.4 Ancient Construction Tools and Techniques 90

7.5 Machines of the Industrial Age 95

Chapter 8: Communication and Information Revolution 100

8.1 Transformative Communication Technologies 100

8.2 Cultural Artifacts of Media History 104

8.3 Tangible Media: From Typewriters to Vinyl 107

Chapter 9: Cultural Expressions Through Fashion 113

9.1 Fashion as Historical Mirror 113

9.2 Fashion Innovators and Icons 117

9.3 Artifacts of Fashion's Future 119

Chapter 10: Symbols and Memory 121

10.2 Memorializing Human Experiences 126

10.3 Symbols Shaping the Collective Imagination 128

10.4 Time Capsules and Commemorative Objects 129

Conclusion 134

Introduction

"The purpose of art is washing the dust of daily life off our souls." — Pablo Picasso

Every object crafted by human hands—be it a chipped stone tool, a woven fabric, or a sprawling fresco—carries a whisper of our shared story. Not just the story of who we are, but how we came to be. These creations are far more than relics; they are the physical expressions of thought, struggle, belief, and beauty. They form a mosaic of what it has meant, across millennia, to be human.

The pages that follow in *The Ultimate Collection of Cultural Artifacts: A Chronicle of Humankind's Greatest Achievements* are not merely a catalog of objects. They are a **testament to humanity's ability to transcend survival through expression**. They trace the arc of civilizations through tools, texts, and traditions that outlived their makers. Whether chiseled in stone, cast in bronze, or coded in silicon, each artifact captures the moment when an idea took shape—and endured.

Why Artifacts Matter

We often think of history as a timeline: events, names, dates. But artifacts tell a more intimate version of the past. A wheel fragment speaks not of abstract technological progress, but of a person's effort to move something heavy more easily. A painted shard of pottery isn't just art—it's evidence of a hand that held a brush, of a meal shared, a culture thriving. Every artifact is **a frozen decision**, a preserved act of creativity or necessity, that links us directly to the intentions and imaginations of those who came before.

In that sense, cultural artifacts are not about nostalgia. They are **tools of understanding**. They reveal how we have confronted mortality, recorded knowledge, represented divinity, entertained one another, and built societies from scratch. They also show that progress is rarely linear—it's layered, regional, interrupted, and often deeply personal.

A Global Tapestry

This book spans centuries and continents, unbound by the notion that history belongs to one region, one empire, or one narrative. Cultural achievement has always been **distributed**, and sometimes its most powerful expressions arise in unexpected places: in the anonymous design of an Incan rope bridge, in a Ghanaian kente cloth, or in the rhythmic echo of a Polynesian chant.

What binds these diverse artifacts is not the material they're made of, but the **intent behind their creation**. Across cultures, people have invented instruments to explore the cosmos, crafted symbols to express collective identity, and built monuments to defy time. This book moves through the ages—from stone tools to skyscrapers, from cave paintings to digital code—connecting these moments of genius in a cohesive and continuous narrative.

Humanity in the Hands of Makers

Every chapter focuses not only on the objects themselves but also on the people behind them: inventors, artists, scribes, engineers, poets, dreamers. A Gutenberg press is not just a machine—it's a revolution in the hands of a man who believed knowledge should be shareable. A Stradivarius violin carries within it not just the resonance of wood and string, but the legacy of a luthier whose precision transformed sound into sublime emotion.

And let us not forget the anonymous creators: the stoneworkers who built Machu Picchu without mortar, the medieval illuminators who spent years crafting manuscripts they might never see completed, the textile weavers who turned raw fiber into cultural identity. The value of an artifact is not determined by fame, but by the **depth of its connection to the human spirit**.

Memory, Meaning, and the Material World

Artifacts act as **memory anchors**. They are how we remember what we cannot witness, how we preserve what would otherwise dissolve. The Rosetta Stone didn't just unlock ancient Egyptian writing—it reminded us that language is translation, and translation is understanding. A commemorative coin minted during war tells us not only about conflict, but about how people endured it, and what they hoped the future might remember.

These objects are not always loud. They do not all glitter. Some are broken, unfinished, or obscure. Yet their power lies precisely in their ability to **collapse time**—to reach across centuries and spark recognition. They carry the fingerprints of their makers, the wear of their users, and the interpretations of every person who encounters them.

In the digital age, when media and messages vanish as quickly as they appear, these tangible pieces of the past carry a different kind of gravity. They ask us to pause, to reflect, and to listen to the **long conversation of humanity**. They remind us that permanence is a choice—and that what we choose to preserve says as much about us as what we create in the first place.

What You'll Discover

Each chapter in this book centers on a theme—whether it's technological innovation, religious expression, literary transformation, or architectural wonder. Within these themes, we've curated artifacts that mark turning points or define a particular cultural moment. The selections are not exhaustive. They are representative. They were chosen to open doors, to provoke curiosity, and to showcase the many forms greatness can take.

You'll begin in ancient times, where invention often emerged from survival—wheels, writing systems, and the earliest attempts to chart the heavens. From there, the journey moves into the grandeur of empires carved in stone and marble, through revolutions in art, language, music, and science. By the time you arrive at the final chapters, you'll encounter the objects of remembrance and symbolism—those that look backward, forward, and inward.

Though the layout is thematic, not strictly chronological, you'll feel the **evolution of culture**. You'll see how one idea inspired another. How tools evolved into machines. How faith inspired art. How resistance became its own form of expression. How one person's vision could ripple into an entire era's identity.

An Invitation to Reflect

This book is not just for scholars or historians. It's for **anyone who has ever looked at an old photo, a worn-out ticket stub, or a fading letter and felt its**

weight. You don't need a degree to recognize that a poem can be a revolution, that a melody can carry a culture, or that a clay tablet can contain the roots of science.

It's also an invitation to reconsider the artifacts of today. What will future generations find valuable in our lives? Will it be a protest banner? A solar panel? A digital archive? What messages are we leaving, intentionally or not?

Our ancestors didn't always know what would endure. They built and painted and wrote because they had to—because it was how they made sense of the world. Some of their creations crumbled. Others, by design or accident, survived. And those survivors are the bones of our cultural memory.

This book is your guided walk through the **museum of humanity**, not behind a glass pane, but within reach. You're invited to hold each item with your imagination, to see not only its surface but the invisible threads it weaves through time. With each turn of the page, you're stepping into a story far larger than any one era or individual—a story written in stone, ink, fiber, metal, and memory.

Welcome to *The Ultimate Collection of Cultural Artifacts*.

This is not just a book about what we've made.

It's about who we are—and who we're still becoming.

Chapter 1: Echoes from Antiquity

"Time crumbles things; everything grows old under the power of Time." — Aristotle

1.1 Ancient Innovations that Shaped Civilization

Before the pyramids pierced the sky and long before empires sprawled across continents, there were moments of quiet brilliance—decisions and inventions so practical and profound that they changed the very structure of human life. While much of early human history was shaped by survival—hunting, gathering, adapting to climate and terrain—it was these early innovations that pushed civilization out of the cave and into the world.

Some of these breakthroughs seem so basic today that it's hard to imagine a world without them. Yet, in their time, they represented bold new ways of understanding and manipulating the environment. The wheel, the written word, and the calendar are three such marvels—fundamental not just to society, but to how we think, move, and organize the world around us. These weren't isolated strokes of genius. They were the slow result of generations of trial and error, observation, and imagination.

The Wheel: The Engine of Progress

It's hard to overstate how revolutionary the wheel was—yet its origins are surprisingly humble. Not invented for transport, as many assume, the earliest wheels appeared as **potter's wheels** around 3500 BCE in Mesopotamia. Here, the innovation was not mobility, but rotation: a symmetrical, efficient way to shape clay. This simple circular platform would spin under the artisan's hand, allowing for smoother, faster pottery production. But this modest utility sparked a far greater realization—if circular motion could ease labor in one context, could it do the same elsewhere?

Applying the concept to transportation required additional breakthroughs. Wheels needed to be paired with **axles**, and those axles had to turn in tandem without breaking under pressure. Early carts were likely clunky and inefficient, but over time, they evolved—wooden discs carved from planks, later reinforced with copper or bronze fittings. Around 300 years after the potter's wheel emerged, the first wheeled vehicles appeared in the archaeological record, most notably in Sumer and Central Europe.

From there, the wheel went global. It became the literal and symbolic engine of progress—**chariots racing across battlefields**, **carts carrying crops**, and **wagons opening trade routes** across great distances. Entire civilizations began to grow around the ability to move more, faster. With wheels came roads, with roads came trade, and with trade came cultural exchange, shared language, and the diffusion of ideas.

But the genius of the wheel lies not just in its physical presence, but in its **conceptual leap**. It represents abstraction—the idea of harnessing natural forms (like circular motion) for structured utility. It's a bridge between geometry and engineering, between observation and execution.

The wheel also transformed how people understood **effort** and **distance**. It reduced the limitations of terrain. Suddenly, landlocked communities could become connected hubs; river valleys became highways. Goods once carried on backs could now be hauled in bulk, expanding economies and even social hierarchies.

Without the wheel, there could be no carts, no gears, no pulleys, no watermills, no mechanical clocks, no industrial engines. Its essence is everywhere—in timepieces, turbines, even the hard drives of our digital age. It is, perhaps, the most quietly omnipresent artifact in human history.

Writing Systems: Memory Made Visible

If the wheel allowed humans to move through space, **writing** allowed us to move through **time**. It is humanity's earliest attempt at external memory—turning thought into matter, speech into symbol, fleeting experience into something enduring.

The earliest known writing systems emerged independently in different parts of the world, with **Sumerian cuneiform** in Mesopotamia and **Egyptian hieroglyphics** often cited among the first. Cuneiform, dating back to at least 3200 BCE, began not as narrative or poetry, but as **accounting**—a system of marks to track goods, debts, and ownership. Pressed into wet clay with a stylus, these wedge-shaped impressions became the administrative backbone of early city-states. Hieroglyphics, likewise, began with sacred and royal inscriptions, carved into temple walls and monuments, emphasizing lineage, divinity, and political power.

Despite their different origins, early scripts shared a common function: **to fix meaning**. Oral traditions are rich and vital, but they shift with each retelling. Writing offered permanence—and with it, the potential for legal codes, historical chronicles, religious texts, and literature.

Over time, writing systems became more refined and expressive. In Mesopotamia, cuneiform adapted to capture myths and philosophies, including the *Epic of Gilgamesh*, one of the world's oldest surviving literary works. In Egypt, scribes developed cursive hieratic and demotic scripts for more everyday use, while monumental hieroglyphs remained tools of ceremony and power.

Other ancient civilizations developed their own writing systems. The **Indus Valley script**, still undeciphered, hints at a complex society with administrative knowledge. In China, **oracle bone inscriptions** from the Shang Dynasty (circa 1200 BCE) show writing used for divination and record-keeping. The **Mesoamerican scripts**, especially that of the Maya, combined logograms and phonetic symbols to record history, astronomy, and ritual with astounding intricacy.

Writing democratized slowly. For centuries, it was the domain of scribes, priests, and royalty. But its spread allowed societies to grow in complexity. It enabled **bureaucracy**, **law**, **education**, and **memory across generations**. Writing preserved not just events but ideas. With it, humans began to build civilizations not just from stone, but from sentences.

Writing is perhaps the most durable of all human inventions. Even when languages fade, their scripts can endure, waiting to be decoded. Clay tablets survive where palaces do not. Inscriptions carved into forgotten monuments are often the only clues we have of a civilization's existence. Writing turned impermanence into legacy.

Calendars: Mapping Time and Meaning

If writing made it possible to record time, **calendars** made it possible to live by it.

The calendar is one of humanity's earliest attempts to impose order on the cosmos. From the moment people began to cultivate land and observe the skies, they noticed **patterns**—the phases of the moon, the movement of the sun, the shifting of stars. These rhythms shaped their survival: planting, harvesting, hunting, celebrating, mourning. Over time, those rhythms were **measured**, codified, and institutionalized.

The earliest calendars were deeply entwined with **astronomy and religion**. The **Egyptian calendar**, one of the first solar systems, was based on a 365-day year and closely tracked the flooding of the Nile—a crucial event for agriculture. Egyptian priests noted that the heliacal rising of **Sirius**, the brightest star in the sky, preceded the inundation. This celestial event became not just a seasonal marker, but a sacred symbol of rebirth.

In **Mesopotamia**, the **Babylonians** developed a sophisticated **lunisolar calendar**, combining lunar months with adjustments to align with the solar year. They tracked planetary movements with astonishing accuracy, even predicting eclipses. Their calendar had not only practical but cosmological significance—linking divine order with civic planning.

The **Mayan calendar**, a marvel of mathematical and astronomical knowledge, used a complex system of interlocking cycles, including the **Tzolk'in** (a 260-day ritual calendar) and the **Haab'** (a 365-day solar calendar), as well as the **Long Count**, which tracked time over millennia. For the Maya, time was not linear—it was cyclical, imbued with sacred repetition.

Across the world, other systems emerged. The **Chinese calendar**, based on lunar and solar cycles, included zodiac animals and five elements, blending astronomy with philosophy. In ancient India, the **Panchanga** combined lunar months with solar years, aligning religious festivals with celestial positions.

Calendars were more than tools to tell the date—they were **blueprints of worldview**. They mapped **the relationship between humans and the cosmos**, between society and the divine. They structured rituals, legitimized kingships, and regulated life from cradle to grave.

In time, calendars became tools of empire and standardization. The **Julian calendar**, introduced by Julius Caesar in 46 BCE, attempted to bring regularity to Roman civic life, replacing the earlier, irregular Roman lunar calendar. It was later corrected by Pope Gregory XIII in 1582 with the **Gregorian calendar**, which most of the world uses today. But beneath the modern months and weekdays lies the echo of ancient observation: a connection to the stars, the seasons, and the turning of the Earth.

These three innovations—the wheel, writing systems, and calendars—did not emerge overnight. They were born from **necessity**, refined by observation, and preserved through culture. They allowed humans not only to survive but to coordinate, to create, and to imagine futures beyond immediate needs.

They are not just inventions. They are **frameworks**—for movement, for memory, for meaning.

And they remain with us. We ride bicycles and send rockets using the same principles of the wheel. We write emails and legal contracts, novels and algorithms, as extensions of early scribes' marks. We set alarms, schedule meetings, and celebrate New Year's based on systems first tracked by priests watching stars in the night sky.

In these ancient innovations, we find the roots of our modern world. And more importantly, we find ourselves—still turning wheels, still writing stories, still watching the sky for a sense of when and where we are.

1.2 Artifacts of Faith and Belief

Humanity has always looked beyond the material world to search for meaning in the mysterious. Long before formal doctrines or organized religions took root, people crafted objects to communicate with forces they could not see—to honor the dead, to invoke fertility, to explain the unexplainable. These artifacts of faith and belief are not merely religious tokens; they are tangible manifestations of deep existential yearning. Through them, we gain insight into the spiritual lives of people who lived thousands of years ago—their fears, their hopes, and their vision of what lies beyond death or beneath the stars.

Some of these artifacts were never meant for public view. Others were designed as grand displays of power intertwined with divinity. Whether subtle or monumental, they reflect the ways humans have consistently merged art with belief. Among the most illuminating of these sacred objects are the *Egyptian Book of the Dead*, the *Terracotta Army* of China, and the mysterious *Venus figurines* from prehistoric Europe.

The Egyptian Book of the Dead: A Roadmap to Eternity

In ancient Egypt, death was not an end but a passage into another realm—a journey through the underworld where the soul would be tested and judged before reaching its final destination. To navigate this perilous afterlife, Egyptians developed a guidebook: a sacred text known today as the *Book of the Dead*.

More accurately a collection than a single work, the *Book of the Dead* was a compilation of spells, prayers, hymns, and instructions meant to assist the deceased in their transition from mortal life to the eternal fields of the blessed. These texts were inscribed on **papyrus scrolls**, tomb walls, and even coffins, often accompanied by detailed illustrations depicting gods, demons, and symbolic landscapes.

The origins of these funerary texts trace back to the *Pyramid Texts* of the Old Kingdom (circa 2400 BCE), which were reserved for royalty. Over centuries, these writings evolved through the *Coffin Texts* of the Middle Kingdom and finally into the more democratized *Book of the Dead* during the New Kingdom (circa 1550 BCE). What was once exclusive to kings became available—albeit still at a price—to high-ranking officials, priests, and the wealthy elite.

One of the most iconic images from the *Book of the Dead* is the **"Weighing of the Heart"** scene. In it, the deceased's heart is weighed against the feather of Ma'at, the goddess of truth. If the heart was heavier—signifying a life burdened by sin—it would be devoured by Ammit, a fearsome creature part lion, part crocodile, part hippopotamus. If the scales balanced, the soul was welcomed into the afterlife.

The *Book of the Dead* reveals a civilization obsessed not with death, but with continuity. Egyptians believed the afterlife was a mirror of earthly life, requiring preparation, provisions, and spiritual guidance. These texts were not just ritual; they were **manuals for immortality**, created by a society that mastered writing not only for bureaucratic precision but also for metaphysical navigation.

Today, fragments of the *Book of the Dead* survive in museums across the globe. They serve as haunting, beautiful reminders that for the ancient Egyptians, the journey beyond death was a sacred extension of life—and that words held the power to carry a soul across eternity.

The Terracotta Army: Guardians of Imperial Immortality

In 1974, a group of farmers digging a well near Xi'an, China, unearthed fragments of what would become one of the most extraordinary archaeological finds of the 20th century: the **Terracotta Army**. Buried for over two millennia, this silent army was created to accompany **Qin Shi Huang**, the first Emperor of China, into the afterlife.

More than **8,000 life-sized clay soldiers**, along with horses, chariots, and acrobats, have since been uncovered in a vast necropolis stretching over 20 square miles. Each soldier has distinct facial features, hairstyles, and armor, reflecting different military ranks and ethnic identities within the imperial forces. Crafted with astonishing realism, they appear less like mass-produced sculptures and more like portraits—frozen in formation, forever guarding their sovereign.

This monumental endeavor was more than a display of imperial vanity. It was rooted in **a deep belief in continuity after death**. Like the Egyptians, the early Chinese believed the afterlife mirrored earthly existence, and that status, wealth, and protection must be preserved in the next world. But where the Egyptians relied on texts and amulets, the Qin dynasty used scale, labor, and an unparalleled devotion to detail.

Constructing the Terracotta Army required massive resources: an estimated 700,000 workers toiled over decades to complete it. Workshops specializing in heads, torsos, and weaponry suggest an assembly-line efficiency coupled with master craftsmanship. The warriors were originally painted in vivid colors—reds, blues, and greens—though much of the pigment has faded with time.

More than an army, the complex included **bureaucrats, entertainers, and animals**, hinting at an afterlife that wasn't only about defense but governance and leisure. It was an entire imperial court reborn in clay.

The Terracotta Army stands as a testament to the fusion of **power, belief, and artistic ambition**. It demonstrates how rulers sought to project their dominance into eternity—not only through monuments of stone but through the sculpted faces of their imagined eternity.

Venus Figurines: Icons of Mystery and Fertility

Long before written language or organized religion, small carved figures began to appear in Ice Age Europe, scattered from the Pyrenees to Siberia. These **Venus figurines**, dating as far back as 30,000 BCE, are among the earliest known representations of the human form.

Though varying in size and style, most Venus figurines share distinctive features: exaggerated breasts, hips, thighs, and abdomens, often with little attention paid to facial detail or limbs. The most famous of these is the **Venus of Willendorf**, discovered in Austria in 1908. Barely four inches tall, she is crafted from limestone and tinted with red ochre, possibly symbolizing life or menstruation.

Interpretations of these figurines abound. Some scholars view them as **fertility idols**, representations of motherhood or abundance. Others argue they may have served as **amulets**, used in rituals or as talismans for safe childbirth. Some suggest they represent idealized forms of femininity, or even early expressions of self-awareness and identity.

Whatever their purpose, these figures reveal a prehistorical reverence for the **female body as a vessel of creation**. They reflect an early spirituality rooted not in gods or temples, but in **life itself**—in the cycles of birth, nourishment, and continuity. The Venus figurines were portable, tactile, and likely intimate. They weren't built to awe crowds or immortalize rulers. They were for hands, not halls—for rituals whispered, not proclaimed.

Together, the *Book of the Dead*, the *Terracotta Army*, and the *Venus figurines* show that belief is not only spoken or preached—it is sculpted, inscribed, buried, and carried. These artifacts offer windows into inner worlds—of individuals and cultures alike—revealing the profound ways that humans, from the earliest times, have tried to connect with the unknown.

1.3 Wonders Lost and Found

Some artifacts live in museums. Others lie buried, waiting. And a rare few exist in the public imagination more than in the physical world—haunted by the sense that they were lost before they could be fully understood. The most fascinating relics are often those that **straddle the line between myth and material**—

objects that reveal entire dimensions of ancient knowledge, only to raise more questions than they answer.

In this section, we explore three such enigmas: the *Antikythera Mechanism*, a device that hints at ancient Greek genius far ahead of its time; the *Dead Sea Scrolls*, which revolutionized our understanding of early religious texts; and the *Library of Alexandria*, whose very loss has become a symbol of cultural tragedy.

The Antikythera Mechanism: The Analog Computer of Antiquity

Discovered by sponge divers off the coast of the Greek island of Antikythera in 1901, this corroded bronze artifact didn't look like much at first—just a lump of metal and wood recovered from a sunken Roman shipwreck. It took decades, and the advancement of X-ray technology, before researchers realized what they had: a complex assembly of gears, dials, and inscriptions now known as the **Antikythera Mechanism**.

Dating to around 100 BCE, the device was used to **predict astronomical events**—eclipses, planetary positions, and even the timing of the Olympic Games. Its internal mechanics include at least 30 interlocking bronze gears, operating with a sophistication that wouldn't be seen again until medieval clockwork more than a thousand years later.

This is not simply an artifact—it is a revelation. The Mechanism challenges our assumptions about ancient technology. It suggests that Greek engineers possessed a far more advanced understanding of **mechanics, mathematics, and astronomy** than previously believed. The device operated as a kind of **hand-cranked analog computer**, using gear ratios to model the movement of celestial bodies with remarkable accuracy.

And yet, no other devices quite like it have been found. Was this a one-off invention? Or part of a now-lost tradition of Hellenistic engineering? Its isolation only deepens its mystery.

The Dead Sea Scrolls: Words Hidden in the Desert

In 1947, a Bedouin shepherd stumbled upon clay jars in a cave near the Dead Sea. Inside were parchment and papyrus scrolls—aged, fragile, and covered in Hebrew script. Over the next decade, more than **900 scrolls** were discovered in 11 caves around Qumran, forming what we now call the **Dead Sea Scrolls**.

These texts include some of the oldest known manuscripts of the **Hebrew Bible**, dating from the 3rd century BCE to the 1st century CE. They also include sectarian writings, apocalyptic visions, community rules, and psalms never before seen. The scrolls provide an unparalleled glimpse into **Jewish religious life**, thought, and diversity during a critical era of transition—from Temple Judaism to the foundations of Christianity and Rabbinic Judaism.

Scholars continue to debate the identity of the scrolls' authors—most often believed to be the **Essenes**, a Jewish sect that rejected mainstream Temple practices and lived in ascetic community. Whoever they were, their texts reveal a world of **spiritual ferment**, prophetic urgency, and theological experimentation.

The Dead Sea Scrolls are not just significant for biblical studies—they are a **literary and philosophical treasure trove**. Written in Hebrew, Aramaic, and Greek, they demonstrate the interplay between oral tradition and written scripture, between mysticism and law, between identity and exile.

The Library of Alexandria: A Dream in Ashes

No place in history quite captures the romantic tragedy of lost knowledge like the **Library of Alexandria**. Established in the 3rd century BCE under the Ptolemaic dynasty, it was conceived as a repository for all human wisdom—housing texts in every language, on every subject, collected from across the known world.

Accounts vary, but the library may have contained **hundreds of thousands of scrolls**—scientific treatises, philosophical works, religious texts, poetry, historical accounts. Scholars from across the Mediterranean gathered in Alexandria to study and debate. It was not just a building—it was **an institution**, the ancient world's greatest experiment in universal knowledge.

And then, slowly and tragically, it disappeared. Fires, wars, neglect—its precise fate remains unclear. Was it Julius Caesar's troops who first set it ablaze? Did later Christian or Muslim rulers destroy what remained? Or was it simply lost through the slow erosion of political instability and indifference?

Today, not a single scroll survives. Yet the Library of Alexandria has become a symbol of **what could have been**—a haunting reminder of the fragility of memory, and of how easily centuries of learning can vanish in flame or dust.

From clay tablets buried in desert caves to machines lost beneath the sea, from volumes burned in forgotten halls to figures carved in the image of gods, these artifacts tell stories of knowledge **gained, hidden, preserved, and lost**. They are a testament not only to human creativity, but to the **fragile, astonishing miracle of memory itself**.

1.4 Tools of Survival and Daily Life

Stone Hand Axes, Obsidian Blades, Bone Needles and Fish Hooks

Before the rise of cities and empires, before the written word and monumental architecture, humankind's journey was marked by smaller, quieter revolutions. These were the humble inventions that allowed early humans not only to survive but to slowly, generation by generation, push back the boundaries of the possible. In this chapter, we turn our attention to a trio of artifacts that, while modest in appearance, were nothing less than lifelines: the stone hand axe, the obsidian blade, and the bone needle and fish hook. Each of these tools tells a story of adaptation, ingenuity, and the deep interconnection between human beings and the natural world.

The Stone Hand Axe: Humanity's First Multitool

The hand axe, often considered the "Swiss Army knife" of early humanity, is one of the earliest known tools produced by our ancestors. Its design is deceptively simple—a symmetrical, teardrop-shaped chunk of stone, sharpened along its edges—but its creation represented a major leap forward in cognitive and motor skills.

These tools first emerged during the Lower Paleolithic period, roughly 1.7 million years ago. While simple flake tools predate them, the hand axe shows a new level of intentionality. Rather than simply chipping off a sharp edge, early humans shaped these axes symmetrically, often refining them with astonishing precision. It's not just what the tool could do—it's that it showed someone cared about how it looked and worked.

Made typically from flint, basalt, or other fine-grained stones, hand axes served multiple functions. They could be used for butchering animals, digging for tubers, chopping wood, or breaking bones to access nutrient-rich marrow. In a time when survival depended on being able to quickly adapt to changing environments, such a versatile tool was invaluable.

But beyond function, the hand axe also hints at the beginning of human aesthetics. Some examples from sites like Olorgesailie in Kenya are so symmetrical and carefully shaped that it's hard to believe they were made solely for utility. Archaeologists speculate that they may have also held social or symbolic significance—perhaps even serving as a kind of early calling card or status symbol, showing off the maker's skill.

What's particularly remarkable is the longevity of the design. Hand axes were used for over a million years with relatively little modification. This wasn't because people lacked imagination, but because the tool worked. It's a testament to its timeless design that some archaeologists jokingly refer to it as the "Paleolithic iPhone"—ubiquitous, practical, and surprisingly elegant.

Obsidian Blades: The Cutting Edge of Prehistory

Obsidian, a volcanic glass formed from rapidly cooled lava, is nature's answer to surgical steel. When fractured properly, it breaks along clean, razor-sharp edges that can outperform modern metal scalpels in sharpness. Long before humans learned to smelt iron or forge steel, they were using obsidian to slice, scrape, and sculpt their way through life.

Obsidian blades began appearing in the archaeological record tens of thousands of years ago, and they were especially prominent in areas with volcanic activity, such as present-day Ethiopia, Turkey, and Mesoamerica. What set obsidian apart from other materials was its ability to hold an incredibly sharp edge. A freshly flaked obsidian blade can be just a few nanometers thick at its edge—so sharp it can split cells.

In daily life, these blades were used for everything from processing animal hides to cutting meat and plants. In Mesoamerica, obsidian became particularly revered. The Maya and the Aztecs used it not only for utilitarian tools but also for ceremonial objects, weapons like macuahuitl (wooden clubs edged with obsidian blades), and ritual bloodletting.

Transporting obsidian also became one of the earliest examples of trade. Because good-quality obsidian sources were relatively rare and geographically limited, its presence at distant archaeological sites tells us that ancient humans were already building complex trade networks. A blade found hundreds of miles from the nearest volcano wasn't just a sharp edge—it was proof of human movement, interaction, and exchange.

The act of crafting an obsidian blade itself required skill and knowledge. Napping—a technique of shaping stone by striking it with controlled force—had to be performed with precision. One wrong hit, and the glassy stone could shatter or flake unpredictably. It's a kind of craftsmanship that calls to mind not brute strength, but delicate artistry.

Even today, modern surgeons in some niche medical contexts still use obsidian blades for extremely fine surgical procedures, underscoring how effective this ancient technology remains. It's an eerie and humbling reminder that long before skyscrapers and spacecraft, our ancestors were already working with tools that could rival modern instruments in precision.

Bone Needles and Fish Hooks: Crafting Comfort and Catching Food

If the hand axe and the obsidian blade helped early humans master the land, then the bone needle and fish hook helped them master their environment in more intimate ways—by creating clothing, shelter, and food security.

Let's begin with the bone needle. As early humans migrated into colder regions, the need for protective clothing became essential. Animal hides could keep a person warm, but to be truly effective, they needed to be shaped and stitched. Enter the bone needle—small, delicate, and often beautifully made.

Some of the oldest known needles, dating back over 50,000 years, were discovered in Denisova Cave in Siberia. These slender tools, often no more than a few inches long, were crafted from animal bones such as bird or deer. They feature carefully drilled eyes and fine points, requiring both patience and skill to produce.

What the needle represents is more than just the invention of sewing—it's a sign of advanced planning, care, and social organization. Someone had to hunt or scavenge the animal, someone else had to prepare the hide, and yet another person had to stitch it into usable garments or tents. Sewing is an act of creation, and in many ways, it's an early form of engineering.

The cultural implications are also profound. Sewing allowed early humans to thrive in diverse environments. They could wrap infants securely, keep elders warm, and even craft symbolic garments. The bone needle, then, becomes a quiet but powerful symbol of care, ingenuity, and identity.

Now consider the fish hook. Before agriculture, consistent sources of protein could be hard to come by. Fishing provided a reliable food source, but it demanded a different kind of thinking—understanding tides, currents, and the habits of underwater creatures. The invention of the fish hook represents the transition from opportunistic scavenging to proactive food procurement.

Early fish hooks, dating back around 20,000 years, were typically made from bone, shell, or even carved wood. In some Polynesian cultures, fish hooks were so valued that they were passed down as heirlooms or even buried with the dead. Some were highly stylized, indicating a blend of function and symbolism.

Crafting a fish hook required careful shaping and polishing. The barb needed to be strong enough to hold a wriggling catch but light enough not to deter a bite. It also required knowledge of cordage and baiting techniques. Together with fishing lines made from sinew or plant fibers, these hooks formed part of one of the earliest and most enduring forms of subsistence technology.

Just as the hand axe was the emblem of the hunter and traveler, the fish hook marked the ingenuity of communities tied to rivers, lakes, and seas. It wasn't just about catching fish—it was about understanding ecosystems, reading the water, and making tools that mirrored nature's rhythms.

Small Tools, Big Impacts

When we speak of "greatest achievements," our minds often leap to the dramatic—the soaring architecture of ancient civilizations, the luminous works of art, the breakthroughs of science and philosophy. But greatness is also found in subtlety. In the careful flake of obsidian glass, in the symmetry of a hand axe, in the slender eye of a needle carved from bone, we see a different kind of brilliance: a quiet, persistent innovation driven by necessity, empathy, and observation.

These tools were not just about surviving the elements—they were about mastering them, bending them to human needs without losing sight of nature's logic. Each represents a milestone not only in technological evolution but in the development of culture. They required teaching, imitation, collaboration, and trust. They helped build not just shelters and meals, but relationships and traditions.

In the grand museum of human history, it's easy to overlook these small, utilitarian items. But pause for a moment, and you'll realize: they were the foundation upon which everything else was built.

Before we wrote poetry or built temples, we stitched clothes and sharpened blades. In these actions, humanity began its long, remarkable story.

1.5 Currency and Trade Artifacts

Clay Ledgers and Tokens, Knife Money and Cowrie Shells, Electrum Coins from Lydia

Trade didn't begin with ships or marketplaces. Long before bustling bazaars and international merchant fleets, human beings were already exchanging goods, ideas, and promises. But trade requires more than desire—it requires trust. How can two strangers agree on the value of a basket of grain, or a length of dyed fabric? How do you prove a debt, or tally what's owed? This is where the evolution of currency and trade artifacts becomes not just a story of economics, but one of creativity, social organization, and the earliest forms of record-keeping.

Before coins jingled in purses or paper bills fluttered between hands, trade was tracked in objects—sometimes simple, sometimes beautiful, but always meaningful. In this chapter, we follow the trail of three early systems: clay ledgers and tokens, knife money and cowrie shells, and the dazzling electrum coins from ancient Lydia. Each tells us something essential about how humans began to quantify value, facilitate exchange, and build the very concept of wealth.

Clay Ledgers and Tokens: The Dawn of Accounting

Some 7,000 years ago in the ancient Near East, long before writing was invented, people in the fertile valleys of Mesopotamia faced a new challenge: managing surplus. Agriculture had begun to take root, quite literally, and for the first time, communities could produce more than they immediately needed. Grain, livestock, textiles—these goods began to move not only between neighbors but across growing networks of trade. But how do you remember who gave what, or how much is owed?

These small, shaped pieces—some round like buttons, others shaped like cones, spheres, or cylinders—were made from clay and baked in fire. Each shape represented a specific item or quantity: a cone might mean a measure of barley; a disc might stand for a sheep. When a trade was conducted or a delivery promised, the appropriate tokens were exchanged or stored as proof. It was a proto-accounting system, one of the earliest ways humans began to externalize memory and enforce agreements.

But this system grew more sophisticated. Instead of handing over a bag of tokens, people began sealing them inside clay envelopes, known as **bullae**. These hollow spheres protected the tokens inside and could be stamped or marked with a seal to show authenticity—an early form of notarization. To remember what was inside without breaking them, scribes began pressing the token shapes into the outer surface of the bullae. Over time, these impressions became stylized symbols, giving rise to the earliest written numerals and, eventually, full-fledged writing systems like cuneiform.

These tokens and ledgers weren't just tools—they were the seeds of civilization. They allowed people to trade across distances, plan harvests, and levy taxes. They enabled rulers to govern more than they could personally oversee. The shift from memory to material record-keeping marked a profound leap in human cognition. As clay tablets replaced tokens and symbols became standardized,

Mesopotamian cities like Uruk transformed into economic and administrative powerhouses.

To see a small, thumb-sized clay disc and know that it helped build the foundation for writing, government, and economics is to recognize the subtle genius of early human systems. These tokens may be unimpressive to the modern eye, but they represent a moment when thought first took form in clay.

Knife Money and Cowrie Shells: When Currency Had Character

Across ancient China and parts of Africa and South Asia, trade took on forms that seem strange by modern standards, but were deeply embedded in the cultures that used them. Two of the most curious and influential examples are **knife money** and **cowrie shells**—objects that served as currency while also reflecting the social and symbolic worlds of those who used them.

Imagine reaching into your pocket and pulling out a miniature bronze dagger to pay for your meal. In ancient China, around the 6th to 3rd centuries BCE, this wasn't far from reality. **Knife money**—metal pieces shaped like knives or spades—circulated as currency in regions like Qi and Yan during the Warring States period. These weren't functional weapons, of course; they were stylized representations, often inscribed with the name of the issuing city or ruler.

But why knives? Some historians believe knife money originated as a natural evolution from barter, where tools and blades were commonly exchanged. A blade has intrinsic value—it's useful, hard to make, and durable. Shaping currency to look like a tool could have lent it symbolic weight, reinforcing the idea that it held real, practical value. Over time, these forms became more abstract and standardized, paving the way for the round coins that would later dominate Chinese currency.

Knife money is fascinating not just for its shape, but for what it tells us about early monetary culture. Currency wasn't always meant to be anonymous or plain; it carried local pride, political propaganda, and even artistry. Some surviving examples are finely crafted, with smooth edges and intricate inscriptions—a blend of utility and beauty, commerce and craftsmanship.

On the opposite end of the spectrum, we find the delicate, shiny **cowrie shell**, which became one of the most widespread forms of currency in human history. These small marine mollusk shells were used for millennia across Asia, Africa, and the Indian Ocean trade routes. Lightweight, durable, and naturally attractive, cowries were easy to carry, hard to counterfeit, and widely accepted.

Cowries were especially prized in West Africa, where they became a cornerstone of trade and taxation. Kingdoms like Mali and Benin used cowrie shells for everyday purchases and official accounting alike. Some African societies even maintained complex systems for valuing cowries, with elaborate rules about stringing them, counting them, and storing them in designated containers. They were not merely money—they were part of social ritual, status display, and religious symbolism.

In China, cowrie shells (or imitations made from bone and bronze) were used before the advent of coinage, their use stretching back to the Shang Dynasty. They were often found in graves, signifying wealth and spiritual currency in the afterlife.

What links knife money and cowries is the human instinct to assign meaning to objects—not just for their material worth, but for their symbolic resonance. These early currencies show us that money has never been merely about trade; it's also about culture, belief, and identity.

Electrum Coins from Lydia: The Birth of Modern Money

If clay tokens and cowries were stepping stones, then the electrum coins of ancient Lydia were a leap into a new era: the invention of standardized, government-issued currency. Around the 7th century BCE, in what is now western Turkey, the Lydians began minting coins from **electrum**, a naturally occurring alloy of gold and silver.

These coins, often bean-shaped and stamped with images of lions, bulls, or mythical symbols, were the first in history to carry both a defined weight and a guarantee of value. Their standardization was revolutionary. For the first time, merchants could engage in trade without bartering or weighing out metal. The coin itself was a promise backed by the issuing authority—typically the Lydian king, such as the famously wealthy Croesus.

The impact of Lydian coinage cannot be overstated. It introduced the concept of portable, universally recognized value. It made commerce more efficient, helped build trust across regions, and allowed for the rise of a merchant class. And once the idea took hold, it spread rapidly—first through the Greek world, then to Persia, and eventually across the Roman Empire and beyond.

The Lydian coins were small marvels of metallurgy and design. Some bore two animals facing each other—a lion and a bull—perhaps representing balance or dual power. Others featured intricate geometric patterns. These images weren't just decoration; they served as marks of authenticity and origin, similar to the logos on modern bills and coins.

Moreover, electrum coins reflected an understanding of abstraction. Their value was no longer tied strictly to their weight in precious metal, but to a collective belief in the issuing state's credibility. This paved the way for the even more abstract money of future centuries—banknotes, credit, and eventually digital currency.

From Objects to Systems

Looking at these early trade artifacts, one theme becomes clear: money is never just about metal or shells or clay. It is a **system**—a shared agreement among people to assign and honor value. This agreement requires symbols, enforcement, trust, and imagination.

The clay tokens of Mesopotamia were not just counters; they were the first contracts. The cowrie shells and knife money of Asia and Africa weren't just exotic oddities; they were anchors of culture, chosen for what they represented. And the electrum coins of Lydia were not just bits of shiny alloy; they were a breakthrough in the language of trade—a symbol that value could be created, carried, and trusted across borders.

In a modern world where currency is increasingly invisible—reduced to numbers on screens—it's worth remembering that the foundations of money are tactile, tangible, and deeply human. These artifacts connect us to a time when trade was personal, when every token or coin carried a story, and when the idea of value was still being invented one object at a time.

They may be small enough to fit in a hand, but these early currencies carried the weight of civilizations.

Chapter 2: Masterpieces in Stone and Marble

"Architecture should speak of its time and place, but yearn for timelessness."
— Frank Gehry

2.1 Expressions of Empire and Glory

Throughout history, empires have used architecture not just to build cities, but to broadcast their power. More than functional spaces, monuments became tools of propaganda—statements of dominance, divinity, and cultural identity. These massive structures weren't only made to impress their contemporaries; they were designed to outlive them, to speak for centuries. Temples, amphitheaters, palaces, and fortresses were all part of an imperial language carved in stone.

Among the greatest examples are the Roman Colosseum, Angkor Wat, and the Great Wall of China—each unique, yet all serving the same core purpose: to turn empire into legacy.

The Roman Colosseum: Strength in Spectacle

Standing at the heart of ancient Rome, the Colosseum was more than an arena—it was a stage for the empire's ideology. Built between 72 and 80 CE, it could host up to 80,000 spectators, offering entertainment in the form of gladiator fights, executions, and staged naval battles. These weren't just shows—they were displays of control, strength, and social order.

Its design was an engineering marvel: layered seating that mirrored Roman society, subterranean tunnels that moved people and animals with precision, and architecture that showcased Rome's command of concrete, arches, and vaults. Funded by emperors, these events doubled as political theater—bread and circuses to win public favor and remind citizens who held power.

Angkor Wat: Sacred Geometry and Imperial Faith

In 12th-century Cambodia, the Khmer Empire fused religion and statecraft in Angkor Wat. Originally a Hindu temple and later a Buddhist sanctuary, this vast complex wasn't just a place of worship—it was a cosmic diagram. Its layout mirrored the structure of the universe, with the central tower symbolizing Mount Meru, the spiritual axis of the world.

Built from sandstone and surrounded by a moat, the temple's symmetry and alignment with celestial events show a profound understanding of astronomy and sacred architecture. Its bas-reliefs tell stories from Hindu epics, mixing myth, history, and kingship. For King Suryavarman II, who commissioned it, the temple was a claim to divine legitimacy—his rule written into the cosmos.

Though the Khmer Empire faded, Angkor Wat survived. Today, it remains a symbol of Cambodia's national pride and a monument to spiritual and architectural mastery.

The Great Wall of China: Boundary and Bond

Stretching across deserts and mountains, the Great Wall is one of the most iconic expressions of imperial will. Built over centuries by various Chinese dynasties, especially the Ming, it served as a defense against northern invaders and a bold marker of civilization's edge.

More than a wall, it was a vast military and administrative network—complete with watchtowers, garrisons, and signaling systems. It demonstrated the state's reach, discipline, and ability to mobilize massive labor forces. Thousands of workers, many of them prisoners or conscripts, lost their lives building it.

Paradoxically, the Wall also facilitated exchange. Along its routes, trade passed and cultures mingled. While meant to keep threats out, it became a point of contact as much as division. Its symbolism was clear: here ends the known world, and here begins the empire.

2.2 Temples of the Spirit

Throughout human history, sacred spaces have represented more than places of worship—they have stood as architectural manifestations of humanity's deepest spiritual aspirations. These temples, shrines, cathedrals, and sanctuaries are not only structural marvels but also cultural codices etched in stone, shaped by religious devotion and artistic ingenuity. They communicate eternal truths, express sacred order, and provide a physical locus for the intangible mysteries of existence. Each temple is a unique synthesis of theology, ritual, aesthetics, and engineering, reflecting the spiritual identity of its civilization.

The Parthenon: Geometry in Service of the Divine

Rising proudly atop the Acropolis in Athens, the **Parthenon** is one of the most iconic temples in Western civilization. Completed in **432 BCE**, this grand marble edifice was dedicated to **Athena Parthenos**, the virgin goddess of wisdom and warfare, and the patron deity of the city. Designed by the architects **Ictinus** and **Callicrates**, and adorned by the sculptor **Phidias**, the Parthenon epitomizes classical ideals of balance, proportion, and harmony.

Constructed primarily in the **Doric order**, the Parthenon features subtle refinements that reveal the sophistication of its creators. Its columns are slightly bowed—a technique known as **entasis**—to counteract optical illusions of concavity. The platform on which it stands, the **stylobate**, gently curves upward in the center to create a perfect visual effect. These optical adjustments demonstrate the ancient Greeks' obsession with mathematical perfection and their belief that architectural beauty mirrored cosmic order.

Decorative friezes and pediments depicted mythological scenes, from the birth of Athena to the Panathenaic procession. The famous **Elgin Marbles**, once adorning the Parthenon, captured Athenian identity in motion—celebrating civic unity, military victory, and cultural excellence. These sculptural narratives reinforced the belief that the divine order was not remote, but deeply woven into the city's political and social life.

More than a temple, the Parthenon was a symbol of democracy and the intellectual flowering of **Classical Athens**. It signaled a civilization confident in its ideals, its gods, and its place in the cosmos. Though damaged over centuries by war, looting, and environmental erosion, the Parthenon endures as a cultural beacon and a testament to humanity's pursuit of eternal truth through sacred form.

The Taj Mahal: Love, Loss, and Divine Beauty

Thousands of kilometers east of Athens, in the Indian city of **Agra**, stands another spiritual masterpiece: the **Taj Mahal**. Commissioned by **Mughal Emperor Shah Jahan** in memory of his beloved wife **Mumtaz Mahal**, who died in 1631, the Taj is both a mausoleum and an architectural poem. Constructed between **1632 and 1653**, it reflects the synthesis of **Persian, Indian, and Islamic** architectural traditions, crystallizing centuries of cultural exchange and devotion.

Crafted from luminous white marble and adorned with semi-precious stones, the Taj Mahal's design is a masterclass in symmetry, elegance, and symbolic meaning. Its central dome, flanked by four minarets, rises like a celestial orb over a perfectly square plinth, while the reflecting pools and formal gardens echo the **charbagh** layout described in Islamic visions of paradise.

Calligraphy inlaid with black marble quotes verses from the Quran, inviting reflection on mortality and divine judgment. The floral motifs and arabesque carvings that decorate the inner and outer surfaces evoke the Garden of Eden, while the central tomb chamber bathes in ethereal light filtered through delicate **jali** screens. Everything in the Taj is calculated to lift the viewer's mind from the transience of earthly life to the permanence of the spiritual.

Though born from personal grief, the Taj Mahal has transcended its original purpose to become a symbol of universal love and aesthetic transcendence. Its magnetic pull continues to draw millions annually, who find in its silence a reflection of their own longing for the eternal and the beautiful.

Gothic Cathedrals: Reaching Toward Heaven

In medieval Europe, another form of sacred architecture took shape—**Gothic cathedrals**, vast stone sanctuaries that towered over cities and embodied the spiritual ambitions of Christendom. From the 12th to the 16th centuries, cathedrals such as **Notre-Dame de Paris**, **Chartres Cathedral**, and **Canterbury Cathedral** transformed sacred architecture into theological theater.

Gothic architecture is defined by a set of revolutionary structural innovations: **pointed arches**, **ribbed vaults**, and **flying buttresses**. These features allowed buildings to reach unprecedented heights and admit vast quantities of light through expansive **stained-glass windows**. The effect was more than aesthetic—it was theological. Light symbolized divine presence, and entering a Gothic cathedral was akin to stepping into the heavenly Jerusalem.

Cathedrals were meticulously oriented, often aligned with solstices or feast days, and designed as microcosms of the divine order. Their façades were adorned with saints, prophets, and biblical scenes in sculptural relief, offering illiterate worshippers a visual catechism. Inside, choirs sang sacred polyphony as incense curled into vaulted ceilings, immersing the faithful in a multi-sensory experience of the sacred.

These buildings also functioned as civic and cultural centers. Markets, festivals, and university lectures occurred in their shadows. Cathedrals unified communities, elevated public imagination, and bore witness to the fusion of faith, artistry, and intellect. Even after centuries of decay or damage—such as the fire that ravaged Notre-Dame in 2019—these structures remain pillars of cultural memory and spiritual resonance.

Together, the Parthenon, Taj Mahal, and Gothic cathedrals exemplify the diverse ways in which architecture channels the sacred. Whether through precise geometry, floral ornamentation, or vertical transcendence, these temples of the spirit tell stories of cultures yearning for connection with the divine, the eternal, and the sublime.

2.3 Stone Megaliths and Mysteries

Beyond the grand temples of known civilizations lie structures that defy easy categorization—**megalithic monuments** whose builders left no written records but whose stones speak volumes. These ancient sites, from Stonehenge to Easter Island to Machu Picchu, continue to puzzle and inspire, standing as silent sentinels of spiritual mystery and cosmic alignment.

Stonehenge: Calendar in Stone

Located on **Salisbury Plain** in southern England, **Stonehenge** is one of the world's most enigmatic prehistoric sites. Constructed between **3000 and 2000 BCE**, it consists of concentric circles of massive standing stones, some transported over 200 kilometers. The precise alignment of these stones with the

summer and winter solstices has led many to believe that Stonehenge functioned as an astronomical observatory or ceremonial calendar.

The effort involved in its construction—quarrying, transporting, and erecting stones without wheels or metal tools—suggests a highly organized society with deep spiritual motivation. Burials and ritual objects found nearby indicate that Stonehenge was a sacred landscape, possibly associated with ancestor worship or seasonal rites. Despite extensive study, its exact purpose remains elusive, adding to its enduring allure.

Moai of Easter Island: Ancestors in Stone

In the remote Pacific, the island of **Rapa Nui**—commonly known as **Easter Island**—hosts nearly 900 **Moai** statues, carved between **1400 and 1650 CE** by the Polynesian ancestors of the Rapa Nui people. These massive figures, often weighing over 10 tons, are believed to represent deified ancestors or chieftains, watching over the island's clans from their platforms, known as **ahu**.

Each Moai is unique, featuring stylized facial expressions and elongated forms that reflect a deep spiritual symbolism. The carving and transportation of these statues over rugged terrain remain engineering mysteries. The eventual halting of Moai production and the toppling of many statues may reflect internal social upheaval, ecological strain, or shifts in religious practice.

Yet the Moai remain powerful symbols of ancestral reverence, craftsmanship, and cultural resilience. Their weathered faces continue to face inland, reminding us that spiritual traditions often arise from a deep connection to the land and community.

Machu Picchu: Sacred City in the Clouds

High in the Peruvian Andes, the lost Incan city of **Machu Picchu** was built around **1450 CE** and abandoned roughly a century later. Rediscovered by **Hiram Bingham** in 1911, the site has since become a symbol of Incan architectural genius and spiritual reverence.

Machu Picchu consists of agricultural terraces, ceremonial plazas, and temples precisely integrated into the mountainous terrain. The **Temple of the Sun**, for example, is aligned with the June solstice, allowing sunlight to pass through a window and illuminate a ceremonial stone. Such precision suggests that Machu Picchu was a cosmological center as well as a royal retreat.

The city's construction employed advanced stone-cutting techniques, without mortar, yet the stones fit so tightly that not even a blade of grass can slide between them. This engineering feat, coupled with its breathtaking location, evokes a harmonious relationship between human architecture and the natural world.

Machu Picchu's spiritual aura and sophisticated design illustrate the Inca belief that the sacred permeates the landscape—that mountains, rivers, and skies are not just backdrops but living elements of a divine order.

Stones That Speak

From the sacred geometry of the Parthenon to the cosmic alignments of Stonehenge, these temples and monuments express humanity's yearning for meaning, order, and transcendence. Whether designed to honor deities, ancestors, or natural cycles, they embody the universal impulse to connect the material with the mystical. They remind us that long before modern technology, ancient peoples used stone and sky to articulate their place in the universe. In doing so, they left behind sacred messages not only for their gods—but for us.

2.4 Spaces of Civic Life and Public Identity

When we think of architecture as a reflection of culture, we often picture towering temples or mighty fortresses — buildings that symbolize power, belief, or glory. But some of the most revealing and influential structures in human history have been the ones designed not for gods or kings, but for ordinary people. Public spaces like forums, agoras, amphitheaters, and marketplaces have long served as the beating heart of civic life. They weren't just backdrops to history — they were its stage.

These civic spaces offer a window into how people lived together, how they organized society, and how they gave shape to abstract values like justice, freedom, and community. While they may lack the ornate grandeur of palaces or temples, they more than make up for it in what they represent: the shared experience of being part of a collective, the lived reality of citizenship, and the rhythm of everyday public life.

The Greek Agora: Democracy in Action

In ancient Greece, the **agora** wasn't just a marketplace — it was the nucleus of public life. Located at the center of the city, it functioned as an open-air meeting ground where citizens gathered to shop, debate, worship, and engage in politics. It was both functional and symbolic, embodying the Greek ideal of the *polis* — a self-governed city-state of active participants.

The Athenian Agora, in particular, stands out. It was surrounded by stoas (covered walkways), government buildings, temples, and statues. Here, Socrates is said to have wandered, questioning passersby, challenging assumptions, and planting the seeds of Western philosophy. More than a physical place, the agora represented the soul of Athenian democracy — messy, open, and vibrant.

Every element of the space encouraged civic engagement. Citizens could listen to speeches, vote on laws, witness trials, or just share news. By physically placing governance in the midst of daily life, the Greeks blurred the line between public and private, between individual identity and communal belonging. The architecture didn't just house political life; it *was* political life.

The Roman Forum: Order and Authority in Stone

If the Greek agora was a celebration of democratic dialogue, the **Roman forum** was a demonstration of imperial order. Designed with symmetry and grandeur, forums in Roman cities were highly structured spaces that reflected the Roman obsession with law, hierarchy, and civic pride.

The **Forum Romanum** in the heart of Rome was flanked by basilicas (which served as administrative buildings), temples, and monuments commemorating military victories. At one end stood the Curia, where the Senate met; at another, triumphal arches celebrating emperors' conquests. Statues lined the pathways, narrating Rome's version of history through heroic figures and mythological scenes.

But the forum wasn't just a display of state power. It was also a space for gathering, commerce, and ceremony. Vendors sold goods, citizens mingled, and legal proceedings were held in public view. The integration of sacred, political, and economic life into a single urban space made the forum not only an architectural marvel but a psychological one — a place where Romans were reminded, every day, of their place in the larger structure of the empire.

The layout, the scale, and even the materials used (imported marble from conquered lands) all served to reinforce the might of the Roman state. The forum was a performance — of control, of culture, of continuity.

Amphitheaters and Theaters: Art, Spectacle, and the Public Gaze

While forums and agoras focused on governance and commerce, other public spaces were dedicated to performance, storytelling, and spectacle. **Amphitheaters** and **theaters** were not simply places to watch a show — they were where societies held up a mirror to themselves.

The Greeks built open-air theaters into hillsides, like the famed **Theatre of Epidaurus**, celebrated for its perfect acoustics and harmonious proportions. These theaters hosted tragedies and comedies that explored moral dilemmas, human flaws, and divine justice. Watching a play was not a passive activity; it was part of civic education. Drama was a vehicle for collective reflection, often performed during religious festivals attended by entire communities.

The Romans took this concept and magnified it. Their **amphitheaters**, most famously the Colosseum, were massive venues for entertainment that blended politics with popular appeal. Gladiator contests, animal hunts, and naval reenactments served both as entertainment and imperial messaging. They showcased the might of the empire, its reach across continents, and its capacity to impose order — even in the arena.

Attendance was free, sponsored by emperors or elites hoping to win favor. The message was clear: Rome feeds and entertains you; Rome deserves your loyalty. These spaces functioned as both release valves for public tension and instruments of social cohesion. By bringing together tens of thousands of people under a shared spectacle, they reminded citizens — and subjects — that they were part of something larger.

Markets and Bazaars: Economic Heartbeats and Social Crossroads

Markets and bazaars may seem mundane compared to temples and palaces, but they are among the oldest and most enduring public spaces in human civilization. From the **Grand Bazaar in Istanbul** to the **medieval market squares of Europe**, these places were more than centers of commerce — they were engines of culture.

Markets brought together farmers, artisans, travelers, and traders. They were places of exchange, not just of goods, but of languages, stories, ideas, and customs. In cities along trade routes — like Cairo, Samarkand, or Venice — the market became a cultural melting pot, a vibrant space where local and foreign influences mingled.

Market architecture often evolved organically, reflecting the needs of the community. But some were intentionally grand, signaling the prosperity and openness of a city. Covered arcades, domed halls, and caravanserais added layers of function and aesthetic beauty to what might otherwise be a chaotic sprawl.

What's striking is how markets often occupied central real estate in towns and cities. Their prominence reflected the central role of trade in shaping cultural identity. Festivals, announcements, and public debates frequently happened here — the lines between buying and belonging were blurry.

Civic Squares and Plazas: The Stage of the People

In later centuries, public squares became the symbolic and literal center of many urban environments. Think of **Piazza San Marco in Venice**, **Red Square in Moscow**, **Trafalgar Square in London**, or **Plaza Mayor in Madrid**. These open spaces served as platforms for public events — from royal processions and military parades to protests and revolutions.

The power of a plaza lies in its openness. It invites people in. It becomes what the people make of it. In many cases, these squares became stages for defining historical moments — whether joyous or tragic, revolutionary or repressive.

The architecture surrounding these squares often told a visual story: cathedrals, government buildings, statues, and fountains all played a part in framing the public experience. Even the emptiness between the buildings mattered. That emptiness was filled with possibility — for celebration, defiance, remembrance, or simply gathering.

Civic Architecture as Identity

Across cultures, public architecture was not only a practical solution to shared needs — it was also a way of constructing identity. What people built said something about what they valued. Whether it was the Greeks with their egalitarian agoras, the Romans with their ordered forums, or the Ottomans with their bustling bazaars, the architecture of public life reflected the soul of the society that created it.

These spaces were also inherently performative. Even if no formal performance took place, just being present in a public space meant participating in the drama of civic life. You saw and were seen. You learned through observation. You belonged — or didn't.

Civic buildings and spaces invited participation. They didn't just display culture; they produced it. They were where gossip turned into politics, where strangers became communities, and where ideas took flight.

The Afterlife of Civic Spaces

Many of these historic public spaces continue to exist today, though their meanings have evolved. Some are ruins, silent and still. Others remain vibrant — markets still bustling, squares still filled with life.

What connects them all is their ability to adapt. They've hosted festivals, protests, funerals, and coronations. They've welcomed emperors and dissidents alike. They've absorbed the chaos of crowds and the quiet of solitude. Their stones have heard laughter, chants, prayers, and gunshots.

In modern urban planning, echoes of these ancient public spaces remain. Pedestrian plazas, city centers, concert halls, and open-air markets all draw from the same ancient blueprint: make room for people to gather, to share, to see themselves in one another.

Chapter 3: Canvas and Colors – Revolution in Art

"Every child is an artist. The problem is how to remain an artist once we grow up." — Pablo Picasso

3.1 Artistic Movements that Changed Perception

From the earliest cave paintings to digital installations of the twenty-first century, visual art has remained one of humanity's most profound and adaptable forms of expression. It is a medium through which civilizations have documented their fears, exalted their hopes, celebrated their triumphs, and challenged their assumptions. Art is not merely a passive reflection of the world—it is an active agent of change, helping to shape how societies see themselves and each other.

Throughout history, certain artistic movements have emerged as seismic shifts in visual culture. These revolutions in canvas and color did more than redefine aesthetics—they altered how humans perceive reality, identity, time, and emotion. Some movements arose during moments of cultural renaissance, others in times of turmoil. Yet all were responses to their era's intellectual currents, political upheavals, scientific discoveries, and philosophical reimaginings. Among the most transformative of these movements are the **Renaissance**, **Impressionism**, and **Modernism**, including **Cubism**—each radically altering the visual vocabulary of their times.

The Renaissance: The Rebirth of Human Vision

The **Renaissance**, which began in **14th-century Italy** and blossomed through the **15th and 16th centuries**, marks one of the most significant artistic transformations in human history. It was not merely a rebirth of classical antiquity; it was the reawakening of a worldview that centered the human experience, prioritized empirical observation, and celebrated the beauty of nature and reason.

Renaissance artists like **Leonardo da Vinci**, **Michelangelo**, **Raphael**, and **Sandro Botticelli** redefined the role of the artist from mere craftsman to intellectual and visionary. They studied anatomy, perspective, light, and movement with scientific rigor. **Linear perspective**, perfected by **Filippo Brunelleschi** and employed masterfully by artists like **Masaccio**, gave depth and realism to two-dimensional spaces, creating immersive, believable worlds that mirrored the viewer's own experience.

Leonardo's "Vitruvian Man" and his iconic "Last Supper" blend art with scientific inquiry and philosophical reflection. Michelangelo's Sistine Chapel ceiling fused theological narrative with staggering technical prowess, while Botticelli's "Birth of Venus" reimagined mythological themes with elegance and sensuality. This was a period where art, religion, science, and philosophy intersected to elevate the visual arts into a refined instrument of intellectual exploration.

The Renaissance was also deeply influenced by the rise of **humanism**—a philosophical movement that placed human dignity, potential, and rationality at the center of thought. This focus shifted artistic attention from divine abstraction to the tangible beauty and complexity of the human form. In doing so, art became a vehicle for exploring emotion, individuality, and moral depth, setting the stage for every movement that would follow.

Impressionism: Painting the Fleeting Moment

Fast forward to the late 19th century, and a new revolution began brewing in **France**: **Impressionism**. Born out of dissatisfaction with academic conventions and historical realism, Impressionism challenged the very purpose and methods of painting. Instead of carefully constructed, idealized scenes, **Impressionist painters** sought to capture **immediacy**—the way light played on surfaces, the sensation of a passing moment, the essence of experience rather than its photographic precision.

Artists like **Claude Monet**, **Pierre-Auguste Renoir**, **Camille Pissarro**, and **Edgar Degas** pioneered this approach, using rapid brushstrokes, vibrant color palettes, and outdoor scenes painted *en plein air* (in the open air). Monet's "Impression, Sunrise," from which the movement gets its name, is a hazy, luminous view of a harbor at dawn—a fleeting vision rendered in pigment, mood, and atmosphere.

These artists broke away from studios and patronage systems, choosing instead to exhibit independently. Their work was initially ridiculed by critics who derided it as unfinished or careless. Yet their innovations proved enduring, capturing the **ephemeral beauty** of modern life—urban scenes, leisurely afternoons, dance halls, and gardens bathed in shifting light.

Impressionism also marked a democratization of subject matter. No longer restricted to religious or historical themes, art now depicted everyday people and ordinary places. The goal was not to glorify but to observe, to find significance in the mundane and poetry in the passing. The viewer became a participant, invited to interpret rather than be told what to see.

Furthermore, Impressionism reflected the modern world's growing pace and change. The industrial revolution, urban expansion, and the invention of photography all played a role in shaping the Impressionists' priorities. Their work resonates as a visual language for a rapidly modernizing society—a world in motion.

Modernism and Cubism: Deconstructing the Visible World

The momentum of Impressionism carried into the 20th century, but as the modern world became increasingly fragmented and disorienting, so too did its artistic expressions. **Modernism** was not a single movement but a constellation of responses to a world grappling with mechanization, war, psychology, and existential crisis. Central among these was **Cubism**, pioneered by **Pablo Picasso** and **Georges Braque**, which reimagined space, form, and time in radically new ways.

Cubism abandoned the traditional single-point perspective in favor of multiple viewpoints rendered simultaneously. Objects were broken down into geometric shapes, reassembled in abstract compositions that defied linear logic. This was not art imitating life—it was art revealing the limitations of visual perception and the layered nature of reality.

Picasso's "Les Demoiselles d'Avignon" shocked early 20th-century viewers with its jagged lines, distorted faces, and unapologetic challenge to classical beauty. Inspired by **African masks**, **Iberian sculpture**, and **post-impressionist experiments**, the painting marked a turning point—announcing the end of realism as the dominant artistic mode.

Cubism reflected deeper intellectual currents, such as **Einstein's theory of relativity**, which redefined space and time, and **Freud's theories** of the unconscious, which destabilized notions of self and rationality. Artists no longer assumed a unified perspective or a coherent subject; instead, they explored fragmentation, simultaneity, and paradox.

Modernism at large absorbed and extended these ideas across various movements—**Futurism**, **Expressionism**, **Surrealism**, and **Dada**—each responding to the upheavals of modern life in its own idiom. What united them was a shared conviction: that old forms could no longer contain new realities. Art was no longer a mirror—it was a lens, a hammer, a dreamscape.

As the century progressed, artists like **Marcel Duchamp** pushed the boundaries even further. His infamous **"Fountain,"** a porcelain urinal signed "R. Mutt," challenged the definition of art itself. Could context transform an object into meaning? Could irony serve as critique? Duchamp's readymades and conceptual experiments laid the groundwork for postmodern sensibilities, where art questioned not just form but function, authorship, and authenticity.

3.2 Iconic Masterpieces and Their Secrets

Throughout the annals of art history, certain works have transcended their immediate contexts to become enduring cultural touchstones—masterpieces whose resonance spans centuries, continents, and ideologies. These artworks not only captivate with their beauty and technique but also draw us in with layers of symbolism, unanswered questions, and emotional depth. Behind each brushstroke lies a story—of the artist, of the time, and of humanity's perpetual search for meaning.

Perhaps no artwork embodies this enigmatic allure more than **Leonardo da Vinci's Mona Lisa**, one of the most celebrated and analyzed paintings in history. Completed in the early **16th century**, the portrait continues to mesmerize millions with its serene beauty and subtle complexity. Its subject, commonly believed to be **Lisa Gherardini**, a Florentine woman married to merchant Francesco del Giocondo, is portrayed with a poise and presence that transcends portraiture.

Leonardo employed a technique known as **sfumato**—a delicate blending of tones and colors that produces soft transitions and a smoky, atmospheric effect. This method allowed him to create lifelike depth, particularly evident in Mona

Lisa's face and hands. The result is a painting that seems to breathe and think. Her famously elusive smile shifts with the viewer's gaze, while her eyes, masterfully aligned with vanishing points, appear to follow observers around the room.

Beyond its technical brilliance, the **Mona Lisa** remains a source of speculation and intrigue. Her expression has inspired countless psychological interpretations, ranging from theories of hidden sorrow to feminist readings of feminine mystique. Some scholars suggest the portrait encodes mathematical or musical patterns, reflecting Leonardo's deep interest in proportion, geometry, and harmony. Others have argued that elements of the painting suggest esoteric or symbolic meanings, hinting at the artist's complex philosophical worldview. The painting's theft in 1911 and dramatic recovery only amplified its legend. Today, the Mona Lisa's mystique continues to evolve, cementing its status not just as a masterpiece, but as a global cultural icon.

In stark contrast to the quiet restraint of the Mona Lisa, **Vincent van Gogh's The Starry Night** radiates explosive emotional intensity. Painted in **1889**, during his voluntary confinement at an asylum in Saint-Rémy-de-Provence, this work represents one of van Gogh's most expressive and deeply personal creations. The swirling sky, incandescent stars, and brooding cypress trees form a cosmic ballet of motion and light—a dreamscape rooted in turmoil and transcendence.

The **brushwork** in The Starry Night is energetic and raw, revealing van Gogh's emotional state. The sky rolls and twists in exaggerated arcs, while the sleeping village below rests in solemn stillness. The contrast between celestial motion and earthly repose has been read as a metaphor for spiritual longing or existential anxiety. Scholars have debated whether the painting reflects van Gogh's mental illness, mystical beliefs, or scientific curiosity.

Despite his suffering, van Gogh infused the scene with a sense of hope—stars blazing with vitality, heavens vast yet reachable. Some interpret the work as a visual prayer or meditation on the eternal. Importantly, The Starry Night is not a literal rendering of the sky but an imaginative vision: a confluence of memory, mood, and metaphysical reflection. Its enduring appeal lies in its vulnerability and vitality, offering viewers a glimpse not only of the artist's inner world but also of the universal yearning for peace amid chaos.

Few works confront the viewer as directly and powerfully as **Pablo Picasso's Guernica**, painted in **1937** as a response to the Nazi bombing of the Spanish town of Guernica during the Spanish Civil War. Commissioned for the Spanish Pavilion at the Paris World's Fair, this monumental black-and-white canvas measures nearly 12 feet tall and 25 feet wide—a mural-sized scream against the horrors of war.

Guernica does not offer a linear narrative but instead presents a **fragmented nightmare**: a dismembered horse screaming in agony, a bull looming with silent menace, a mother wailing over her dead child, a soldier's severed arm grasping a broken sword. These distorted forms are rendered in sharp, angular geometry, blending **Cubist abstraction** with **Surrealist dislocation**.

The absence of color intensifies the emotional impact, reducing the scene to shades of despair. Picasso masterfully manipulated visual symbols—lightbulbs shaped like eyes, fractured limbs, distorted faces—to evoke chaos, destruction, and human suffering. Guernica is not merely a protest against a specific event but a universal condemnation of war's cruelty. Its message remains relevant, echoing through subsequent conflicts and political movements. Exhibited around the world, the painting became a symbol of resistance and conscience, demonstrating art's potential as a moral and political force.

3.3 Artifacts as Cultural Commentary

While masterpieces like the Mona Lisa, The Starry Night, and Guernica reflect individual genius and specific historical moments, many artworks function more overtly as **cultural commentary**—challenging societal norms, exposing power structures, and giving voice to marginalized perspectives. Artists such as **Banksy**, **Frida Kahlo**, and **Andy Warhol** have used their work not just to reflect culture, but to critique and reshape it.

The elusive street artist **Banksy** has become synonymous with satirical, politically charged art in the public sphere. Emerging in the early 2000s in the UK, Banksy's stenciled graffiti art critiques everything from **consumerism** and **militarism** to **government surveillance** and **social inequality**. His works appear overnight on city walls, abandoned buildings, and even zoo enclosures, transforming everyday spaces into platforms for political dialogue.

Pieces like **"Girl with Balloon"** evoke emotional themes of loss and hope, while others such as **"Kissing Coppers"** or **"Napalm"** directly challenge social taboos and global injustices. The performative nature of Banksy's work—epitomized when "Girl with Balloon" self-destructed upon auction—blurs the line between art, activism, and spectacle. His anonymity further critiques the commercialization of art, questioning the role of authorship, value, and institutional gatekeeping.

Banksy's impact lies not only in his messages but in his method—accessible, ephemeral, and communal. His work invites participation and discourse, reasserting the democratic power of public art to challenge dominant narratives and empower the voiceless.

While Banksy speaks through satire and anonymity, **Frida Kahlo** used deeply personal imagery to explore themes of **identity**, **pain**, and **cultural hybridity**. Working primarily in the early 20th century, Kahlo painted through physical agony and emotional upheaval, transforming her body and life into powerful visual language. Her work is often classified as **Surrealist**, though Kahlo rejected the label, insisting that her paintings were "the frankest expression of myself."

Kahlo's self-portraits—such as **"The Two Fridas"**, **"Self-Portrait with Thorn Necklace and Hummingbird"**, and **"Broken Column"**—convey physical and psychological suffering while asserting female agency and indigenous identity. Her use of vibrant colors, Mexican folk art motifs, and pre-Columbian symbols reflects a profound connection to her heritage and political beliefs. She became involved with leftist politics and used her art to comment on gender roles, colonialism, and social justice.

In a time when women's voices were often marginalized, Kahlo claimed her narrative and image with unapologetic intensity. Her legacy extends beyond art, influencing contemporary feminism, LGBTQ+ rights, and postcolonial discourse. Kahlo showed that the personal is indeed political—and that self-representation can be an act of resistance.

Another titan of cultural commentary is **Andy Warhol**, whose **Pop Art** movement in the 1960s redefined the relationship between art, commerce, and celebrity. Warhol's silk-screened portraits of **Marilyn Monroe**, **Elvis Presley**, and **Mao Zedong**, alongside his repetitions of **Campbell's Soup Cans** and **Brillo boxes**, subverted conventional notions of originality and authenticity.

Warhol treated mass-produced imagery as high art, thereby **democratizing** artistic subject matter. His studio, **The Factory**, became a cultural hotspot where artists, actors, musicians, and countercultural icons mingled. Warhol embraced fame while simultaneously critiquing it, once declaring, "In the future, everyone will be world-famous for 15 minutes."

Through his deadpan persona and mechanized production methods, Warhol raised provocative questions: Is art still art if it's made on an assembly line? What does it mean to be an individual in a society obsessed with branding? By embracing and exposing consumer culture, Warhol offered a mirror to modern society—one filled with repetition, desire, and irony.

3.4 Portable Masterpieces and Everyday Aesthetics

Art has always traveled with us. It lives not only in grand temples or palatial murals but in the objects people carried, used, and cherished in their daily lives. While history often exalts monumental works—cathedrals, sculptures, and frescoes—the truth is that some of the most enduring cultural artifacts are those that fit into the palm of a hand or rest quietly on a table. These works, small enough to move across empires and intimate enough to touch, reveal as much about human creativity as the grandest architectural feats.

In this chapter, we explore a trio of such treasures: the delicately carved ivory diptychs of Late Antiquity, the vibrant painted ceramics that brought color to kitchens and tombs alike, and the exquisitely illuminated manuscripts that turned reading into a sacred, visual experience. These objects were not only functional or decorative—they were bearers of stories, status, and symbolism. They bridged the worlds of art and utility, public grandeur and private devotion.

Carved Ivory Diptychs: Symbols of Status and Piety

In the fading twilight of the Roman Empire, when emperors still ruled from the East and Christianity was transforming the spiritual fabric of the West, a new form of portable art began to flourish: the **carved ivory diptych**. These hinged panels, often no larger than a book, were crafted from elephant tusks and intricately carved with scenes of imperial ceremony, classical mythology, or Christian devotion.

Originally, diptychs were practical objects—two-panel writing tablets connected by a hinge, with wax-coated interiors used for note-taking. But as Roman society became more hierarchical and ceremonial, these utilitarian items evolved into luxurious gifts, especially among the elite. By the 4th and 5th centuries CE, ivory diptychs had become prestigious tokens, given to mark official appointments, legal judgments, or religious milestones.

What sets these diptychs apart is the precision and elegance of their carving. Artists working in major centers like Constantinople, Ravenna, or Rome would render intricate figures, flowing robes, and architectural settings in low relief, achieving a remarkable sense of depth and movement within a shallow space. Emperors were shown triumphing over barbarians, saints raising their hands in blessing, or mythological creatures woven into allegorical scenes. Every surface became a canvas for visual storytelling.

But these works were more than decorative. They were **statements**—about authority, cultural continuity, and spiritual identity. A consular diptych, given to celebrate a new consul's appointment, would display his name in bold lettering and frame him between columns and classical motifs, reinforcing his link to Rome's prestigious past. Later, as Christianity took firmer root, diptychs became devotional, their imagery turning toward saints, angels, and biblical narratives.

Despite their small size, these ivory panels were anything but modest. They required enormous technical skill, as working with ivory was notoriously difficult—too much pressure could crack it, and its fine grain demanded absolute control from the artist. Each diptych was a labor of care and intention, intended to be handled, admired, and remembered.

Today, many of these ivory artifacts survive in cathedral treasuries or museums. Their survival speaks to their value—not just as art, but as relics of cultural transformation. From pagan Rome to Christian Byzantium, from practical object to spiritual offering, the ivory diptych charts the passage of time through beauty carved in bone.

Painted Ceramics: Color, Craft, and Everyday Beauty

If ivory diptychs belonged to the realm of elites, painted ceramics were the art of the many. Found in homes, markets, and temples across centuries and continents, these objects brought color, pattern, and story into everyday life. From an Athenian kylix to a Tang Dynasty bowl, ceramics were not just vessels—they were expressions of culture, social values, and artistic exploration.

The appeal of painted pottery lies partly in its dual nature. It is, fundamentally, utilitarian: it holds wine, oil, grain, or water. Yet it also offers a blank surface for decoration, inviting painters to turn function into expression. Over millennia, ceramic artists transformed simple earthenware into masterpieces, refining their techniques and creating visual languages unique to their time and place.

One of the earliest and most influential ceramic traditions comes from **Ancient Greece**, where potters and painters elevated the medium to an art form. Black-figure and red-figure techniques, developed between the 7th and 5th centuries BCE, allowed for detailed scenes of mythology, athletics, daily life, and warfare. Artists like Exekias signed their vases, suggesting a sense of authorship and pride. These works weren't merely decorative—they were commentaries on society, laden with symbolism, humor, and sometimes biting irony.

Elsewhere, ceramics told different stories. In **China**, during the Tang and Song Dynasties, painted ceramics reached new levels of sophistication. Tang sancai ("three-color") wares used vibrant glazes of green, amber, and white, often depicting horses, dancers, or celestial figures. These pieces adorned the tombs of the elite and celebrated the cosmopolitan spirit of the Silk Road era. Later, the delicate blue-and-white porcelain of the Yuan and Ming periods became one of China's most recognizable exports, fusing Persian design with Chinese craftsmanship and shaping global tastes.

In **Islamic art**, ceramics flourished under different constraints—representational imagery was often restricted, leading artisans to develop astonishing geometric and floral motifs. Lusterware, a technique that gave ceramics a metallic sheen, became a prized art across the Abbasid Caliphate and later in Moorish Spain. These shimmering pieces combined scientific knowledge with spiritual ideals, embodying harmony and balance.

What all these traditions share is an ethos: that **beauty belongs in daily life**. Whether placed on a peasant's table or in a caliph's palace, painted ceramics democratized art. They made the extraordinary part of the ordinary, and they traveled—traded across oceans, imitated, adapted, and cherished. A broken shard of pottery can tell us as much about a vanished world as a monument can. In color and clay, civilizations speak.

Illuminated Manuscripts: When Books Became Jewels

The Ultimate Collection of Cultural Artifacts

Long before printed books, illuminated manuscripts were the gold standard—literally. Painstakingly written by hand, adorned with vivid pigments and precious metals, these manuscripts were sacred objects, intellectual pursuits, and artistic marvels all in one. Whether created in a medieval monastery or a Renaissance scriptorium, the illuminated manuscript represents the union of **word and image, devotion and discipline**.

The tradition of manuscript illumination began in Late Antiquity and reached its peak in the Middle Ages. Monks in Ireland, Italy, and Byzantium copied religious texts—most commonly the Bible or psalms—by hand on vellum or parchment. But they didn't stop at the text. Margins bloomed with vines, angels, fantastical creatures, and gold leaf that shimmered in candlelight. Every capital letter became an opportunity for invention. Entire pages were transformed into meditative artworks.

One of the most famous early examples is the **Book of Kells**, created around 800 CE in an Irish monastery. Its pages are dense with color and symbolism, turning the Gospels into a visual tapestry. Later, during the Gothic and Renaissance periods, manuscripts became more refined and courtly. The **Très Riches Heures du Duc de Berry**, a lavish French prayer book from the 15th century, not only includes religious texts but detailed calendar pages illustrating the seasons, filled with peasants, nobles, and landscapes—a microcosm of medieval life.

But illumination was not restricted to Christian Europe. In the Islamic world, calligraphy became an art of its own. Qur'ans were copied with breathtaking elegance, the script often framed by geometric borders or illuminated with vegetal motifs. In Persian and Mughal traditions, manuscripts also included miniatures—small paintings illustrating poetry, historical narratives, or scientific works. These were not marginal doodles; they were integral to the reading experience.

Illuminated manuscripts took time—often years to complete. They required collaboration between scribes, illustrators, and binders. The pigments were costly, derived from lapis lazuli, gold, and crushed plants. The effort involved meant that owning a manuscript was a sign of wealth, education, and piety. Yet they were also intensely **personal** objects—prayer books passed down through generations, annotated margins bearing the thoughts of long-gone readers.

In an age before mass communication, these books were **portals**—into scripture, knowledge, and imagination. They made reading a multisensory experience, turning the act of turning a page into a moment of wonder.

The Art We Carried

Carved ivory diptychs, painted ceramics, illuminated manuscripts—three forms of expression, wildly different in medium and audience, yet bound by a common thread: the idea that beauty, meaning, and skill should accompany us in life's every corner. These artifacts were not hidden in vaults or locked behind palace doors. They moved through hands, across borders, between generations. They were admired, used, worn, and sometimes broken—each carrying a trace of the people who touched them.

In them, we see a humanity that was not only inventive but also profoundly **attuned to aesthetics**, to storytelling, and to the joy of making. They remind us that art is not only monumental—it is mobile, humble, and often hidden in plain sight.

Whether in the flicker of gold on a manuscript page, the swirl of glaze on a ceramic bowl, or the curve of a saint's robe carved in ivory, we find evidence of lives deeply engaged in the act of **looking**, of **making**, and of **connecting**—across time, space, and culture. These were not just objects. They were experiences. They were, and still are, portable masterpieces.

Chapter 4: Literature's Timeless Voices

"A room without books is like a body without a soul." — Marcus Tullius Cicero

4.1 Books That Shaped Humanity's Conscience

Since the dawn of written language, literature has acted as one of humanity's most powerful tools for reflection, transformation, and cultural continuity. Through words, societies have preserved their histories, imagined their futures, and interrogated the deepest aspects of existence. Literature is not merely entertainment—it is the collective imagination rendered permanent, a dialogue across generations and civilizations. Certain works, emerging from vastly different times and cultures, have transcended their origins to become timeless artifacts of human conscience. They serve as moral compasses, philosophical meditations, and rallying cries for justice, empathy, and self-awareness.

One of the earliest and most enduring literary achievements is **The Epic of Gilgamesh**, a foundational text from **ancient Mesopotamia**, written around **2100 BCE**. This epic poem, inscribed on clay tablets in the wedge-shaped script of **cuneiform**, follows the exploits of **Gilgamesh**, a powerful yet flawed king of **Uruk**. Initially portrayed as a tyrant, Gilgamesh embarks on a transformative journey spurred by the death of his companion **Enkidu**. His quest leads him across vast landscapes and into the depths of human despair and hope, as he seeks to understand mortality and attain eternal life.

The beauty of Gilgamesh lies not only in its narrative but in its universal themes. Questions about friendship, heroism, grief, legacy, and the nature of life and death reverberate through its verses. As Gilgamesh ultimately learns that immortality belongs to the gods and that human beings must find meaning within their mortal lives, the poem delivers one of literature's earliest meditations on existential purpose. The Epic of Gilgamesh continues to resonate precisely because it addresses what it means to be human, a question as urgent today as it was four thousand years ago.

Moving forward in time but no less influential is the body of work attributed to **William Shakespeare**, especially his collected plays known as **Shakespeare's Folio**, published posthumously in **1623**. This folio preserved 36 of

Shakespeare's plays, including tragedies like *Hamlet*, *Macbeth*, and *Othello*, comedies such as *A Midsummer Night's Dream* and *Twelfth Night*, and historical dramas like *Henry V* and *Richard III*. Shakespeare's writing is often celebrated for its poetic brilliance, but its deeper power lies in its psychological acuity and ethical nuance.

Shakespeare's characters are mirrors to our souls—flawed, conflicted, aspirational, and deeply human. Hamlet's indecision, Lear's pride, Macbeth's ambition, and Iago's malice all reveal facets of the human condition. The Bard's exploration of themes such as power, identity, gender, jealousy, betrayal, and justice invites readers and audiences to confront the complexities of moral choice and self-understanding. Shakespeare's language may belong to Elizabethan England, but his insights transcend time, making his works staples of literary education and moral reflection around the globe.

Jumping forward to the 20th century, we encounter a very different kind of masterpiece—**George Orwell's 1984**, published in **1949**. This dystopian novel painted a chilling vision of a future dominated by totalitarian control, surveillance, and propaganda. Orwell's imagined world, ruled by the omnipresent figure of **Big Brother** and the Party's manipulation of truth, introduced concepts that now seem prophetic—**"doublethink," "thoughtcrime," and "newspeak."**

Orwell did not merely craft a nightmare scenario—he offered a profound warning. Written in the wake of World War II and amid the rise of authoritarian regimes, *1984* reflected Orwell's deep concerns about political manipulation and the erosion of personal freedom. The protagonist, **Winston Smith**, embodies the struggle of the individual conscience against oppressive ideology. His doomed rebellion, love affair, and ultimate psychological breakdown illustrate the terrifying power of totalitarianism to not just control actions, but to colonize thought.

1984 remains a cornerstone of modern literature because it compels readers to question authority, to recognize the dangers of complacency, and to value truth in the face of distortion. In an era of digital surveillance, misinformation, and political polarization, Orwell's vision has never felt more relevant.

These three works—*The Epic of Gilgamesh*, *Shakespeare's Folio*, and *1984*—span vastly different epochs and geographies, yet each has shaped human conscience in profound ways. Gilgamesh confronts the limits of human power and the necessity of humility. Shakespeare reveals the infinite complexities of human nature and ethical ambiguity. Orwell warns of the fragility of truth and freedom in a politically manipulated world.

Together, they represent literature's extraordinary capacity to connect us with the past, illuminate the present, and challenge the future. They remind us that reading is not merely an intellectual exercise, but a moral and imaginative act—one that expands our empathy, sharpens our critical faculties, and enriches our understanding of what it means to be human.

Their endurance also speaks to the communal power of storytelling. These books are not just relics; they are living documents that continue to speak to new generations, in classrooms, theatres, homes, and even protests. Through them, the written word proves its resilience and its power to endure beyond empires, technologies, and ideologies.

As we explore further into the legacy of literature in shaping human civilization, we will encounter other seminal works that bridged cultures, sparked revolutions, and dared to imagine radically different ways of living and knowing. But for now, we pause to appreciate how these timeless voices—etched in clay, inked on parchment, and printed in protest—continue to stir the minds and souls of humanity.

4.2 Literary Milestones of Cultural Exchange

Across millennia, literature has served as one of the most powerful instruments of cultural transmission. From sacred texts to imaginative fiction, stories have crossed borders, transcended languages, and bridged civilizations. These literary milestones do more than entertain—they teach, provoke, inspire, and connect. By carrying values, ideas, and philosophies across cultures, they have helped create a global dialogue that continues to evolve. Some of the most influential literary works in this regard—such as the **Gutenberg Bible**, **Don Quixote**, and **One Thousand and One Nights**—have played pivotal roles in shaping collective human knowledge and expanding intercultural understanding.

The **Gutenberg Bible**, produced in the mid-15th century by **Johannes Gutenberg** in Mainz, Germany, is often heralded as one of the most significant achievements in the history of communication. Not only was it the first major book printed using **movable metal type**, but it also marked the dawn of the **printing revolution** in Europe. Before Gutenberg's invention, books were laboriously hand-copied by scribes, usually in monastic settings, and were accessible only to clergy, scholars, and the elite. The process was slow, expensive, and exclusive.

Gutenberg's innovation fundamentally **democratized knowledge**. By dramatically increasing the speed and volume of book production, the printing press lowered the cost of books and made them accessible to a broader segment of society. The Gutenberg Bible, printed in Latin around **1455**, became a symbol of this transformation—not just as a religious text, but as a vessel of linguistic, cultural, and intellectual change.

The printing press catalyzed the **Renaissance, Reformation, Scientific Revolution**, and **Age of Enlightenment** by allowing scholars, theologians, and thinkers to disseminate ideas rapidly and broadly. The ripple effects extended far beyond religion, giving rise to public literacy, new universities, and secular knowledge. As printing spread across Europe and eventually the world, it created pathways for **cultural exchange**, allowing texts to be translated, circulated, debated, and reimagined. The Gutenberg Bible was not just a book—it was a gateway to an interconnected intellectual landscape that transcended borders.

Another transformative work in global literary history is **Don Quixote**, written by **Miguel de Cervantes Saavedra** and published in two parts in **1605** and **1615**. Widely considered the first modern novel, *Don Quixote* is a cornerstone of Western literature, a book whose influence reverberates across continents and centuries. The story follows **Alonso Quixano**, a man so enamored with chivalric romances that he adopts the persona of the knight **Don Quixote** and sets out to revive the ideals of knighthood in a world that no longer recognizes them.

What makes *Don Quixote* so enduring is its **multi-layered narrative structure**, deep psychological insight, and satirical brilliance. Cervantes masterfully deconstructs the romanticized ideals of heroism, juxtaposing illusion with reality. As Don Quixote tilts at windmills and misinterprets peasants for princesses, readers are invited to reflect on the power of perception, the folly of rigid ideals, and the tension between dreams and disillusionment.

Don Quixote became an immediate success, quickly translated into multiple languages and embraced across Europe and Latin America. Its **cultural mobility** helped establish the novel as a **global literary form**, inspiring writers from **Fyodor Dostoevsky** to **Gustave Flaubert, James Joyce**, and **Jorge Luis**

Borges. The book became a bridge between Spanish literature and the wider world, facilitating the **exchange of narrative techniques**, thematic explorations, and philosophical musings across cultures. Today, the term "quixotic" remains a linguistic legacy of Cervantes' enduring impact.

Equally emblematic of cultural transmission is **One Thousand and One Nights**, also known in the West as **Arabian Nights**. This sprawling collection of Middle Eastern, South Asian, and North African folk tales originated from oral traditions and was compiled over many centuries, reaching its written form sometime between the 8th and 14th centuries. The collection's framing device—the story of **Scheherazade**, who tells tales each night to delay her execution—provides a dynamic structure for stories that encompass genres ranging from adventure and romance to moral parable and cosmic myth.

Tales like **"Aladdin," "Ali Baba and the Forty Thieves,"** and **"Sinbad the Sailor"** became iconic after being translated into French by **Antoine Galland** in the early 18th century. These stories captivated Western audiences and sparked a fascination with the East, fueling **Romantic** and **Orientalist** movements in literature and the arts. Yet beyond their exotic allure, the stories of *One Thousand and One Nights* carried deep insights into Islamic culture, gender dynamics, justice, fate, and wisdom.

While the collection has been critiqued for fostering orientalist stereotypes in later Western interpretations, it remains a testament to the **fluidity of storytelling across civilizations**. These tales have inspired countless adaptations, including operas, ballets, films, and novels, reflecting their adaptability and universal appeal. The Nights remind us that storytelling is a shared human endeavor—one that invites imagination, preserves heritage, and builds bridges between seemingly disparate worlds.

Together, the Gutenberg Bible, Don Quixote, and One Thousand and One Nights illustrate literature's potent role in **fostering cultural dialogue**. Whether through the mass production of sacred texts, the birth of the modern novel, or the dissemination of ancient folklore, these works have helped shape a more intellectually integrated and culturally diverse global community.

4.3 Writers Who Challenged Conventions

While many literary works serve as vehicles of tradition, others function as **revolutions in print**. Throughout history, some writers have dared to challenge the status quo, using their pens to critique injustice, unravel psychological complexities, and assert marginalized voices. Among the most transformative of these figures are **Jane Austen**, **Fyodor Dostoevsky**, and **Maya Angelou**—authors who not only redefined literary form and content but also helped reshape cultural and ethical paradigms.

Jane Austen, writing during the late 18th and early 19th centuries, employed a deceptively genteel style to deliver **sharp critiques of gender roles, class privilege, and social hypocrisy**. Her novels—*Pride and Prejudice*, *Sense and Sensibility*, *Emma*, and others—focus on the domestic sphere, courtship, and marriage, yet beneath their surface lies a **radical reappraisal of women's agency** and societal expectations.

Austen's protagonists are often intelligent, spirited women navigating a world that offers them limited autonomy. Through characters like **Elizabeth Bennet** and **Elinor Dashwood**, Austen subverts romantic conventions, presenting marriage not as a fairy-tale conclusion but as a complex negotiation of values, status, and independence. Her subtle irony and acute psychological insight challenge the patriarchal norms of her time, offering a proto-feminist lens that remains relevant in contemporary discourse.

Austen's impact goes beyond literature; her works have inspired feminist scholarship, cultural studies, and adaptations in every conceivable medium. Her refusal to conform to literary and societal expectations has made her a timeless voice for equality, wit, and moral clarity.

In contrast to Austen's elegant restraint, **Fyodor Dostoevsky** plumbed the **darkest depths of human consciousness**. A former political prisoner and devout spiritual thinker, Dostoevsky brought to Russian literature a philosophical intensity unmatched in its time. His major novels—*Crime and Punishment*, *The Brothers Karamazov*, *The Idiot*, and *Notes from Underground*—examine themes such as **free will, guilt, redemption, nihilism, and the existence of God**.

Dostoevsky's characters are not mere literary creations; they are **existential battlegrounds**, engaged in internal struggles that mirror the social, religious, and philosophical crises of the modern world. His narrative techniques—such as polyphony, interior monologue, and moral paradox—anticipated psychological realism and existentialist philosophy. **Nietzsche**, **Freud**, and **Camus** all acknowledged Dostoevsky's profound influence.

By challenging the rational optimism of Enlightenment thinking and exposing the fragility of the human psyche, Dostoevsky paved the way for a literature that embraces complexity, contradiction, and the shadow side of human nature. He taught readers to confront uncomfortable truths and to seek meaning in suffering—a message that continues to resonate.

If Austen redefined the personal and Dostoevsky explored the philosophical, **Maya Angelou** gave voice to the political and the poetic. Born in 1928 in segregated America, Angelou emerged as a **formidable voice for Black identity, womanhood, and civil rights**. Her groundbreaking autobiography, *I Know Why the Caged Bird Sings*, published in 1969, recounts her early life with unflinching honesty—depicting racism, trauma, silence, resilience, and transformation.

Angelou's lyrical prose blends memoir with poetry, creating a style that is both intimate and universal. Her subsequent volumes of autobiography, along with her poetry collections, plays, and public speeches, positioned her as a cultural icon. Her work was deeply informed by her activism—working with **Martin Luther King Jr., Malcolm X**, and global human rights movements.

Through her life and literature, Angelou challenged dominant narratives about race, gender, and history. She asserted the dignity and complexity of Black life and insisted on the transformative power of language. Her ability to speak truth with grace, to turn pain into art, and to claim space for marginalized voices has left an indelible mark on American literature and global human rights discourse.

Collectively, Austen, Dostoevsky, and Angelou demonstrate that literature is not merely reflective—it is **generative**. It reshapes paradigms, opens new moral vistas, and dares to imagine societies more just, more empathetic, and more self-aware. These writers remind us that challenging convention is not an act of rebellion alone—it is an act of **creation**.

Their legacies endure because they dared to ask difficult questions—and answered them with honesty, imagination, and humanity. In reading them, we not only understand their times but begin to see our own world, and ourselves, more clearly.

Chapter 5: The Symphony of Humanity

"Music expresses that which cannot be put into words and cannot remain silent." — Victor Hugo

5.1 Instruments that Transformed Music

Music, perhaps more than any other art form, transcends language and cultural boundaries, resonating with the human spirit in times of joy, sorrow, celebration, and contemplation. At the heart of this universal language lie the instruments—tools of sound through which individuals express emotion, tradition, and identity. Across time, certain musical instruments have not only changed the way music sounds but have also shaped the very trajectory of musical development. Among the most influential of these are the **Stradivarius violin**, the **piano**, and the **electric guitar**—each a transformative force in its era, with cultural and artistic reverberations that continue to this day.

The Stradivarius Violin: A Legacy of Craftsmanship and Myth

Few musical instruments have captured the imagination of musicians and audiences alike as enduringly as the **Stradivarius violin**. Crafted by Antonio Stradivari in Cremona, Italy, during the late 17th and early 18th centuries, these violins are not merely tools for performance—they are revered cultural artifacts, imbued with a near-mythical aura.

Stradivari's meticulous craftsmanship produced instruments of such tonal clarity, richness, and responsiveness that they remain unmatched even centuries later. Only around 500 of these violins survive today, and each is regarded as a masterpiece in its own right. Scientists and luthiers have long attempted to decode the "Stradivarius secret," investigating everything from the varnish composition and wood density to the precise geometric proportions used in their construction. Despite modern technological advances, no replica has fully succeeded in capturing the distinctive voice of a true Stradivarius.

Beyond their technical perfection, Stradivarius violins are associated with a lineage of virtuosity and excellence. Legendary musicians such as Niccolò Paganini, Itzhak Perlman, and Anne-Sophie Mutter have performed on these instruments, drawing on their extraordinary dynamic range and subtle tonal variations to push the boundaries of expressive possibility. The instrument's remarkable ability to mimic the human voice allows performers to convey deep emotion, bringing to life the most nuanced passages of classical compositions.

In many ways, the Stradivarius violin represents the height of traditional craftsmanship meeting artistic aspiration. It symbolizes the fusion of science and soul, offering insight into an era when music, art, and innovation were deeply intertwined. The reverence for Stradivari's instruments today reflects our broader appreciation for the human capacity to create objects of transcendent beauty and function.

The Piano: The Grand Orchestra at One's Fingertips

If the violin is the lyrical voice of Western classical music, the **piano** is its full-bodied orchestra. Capable of both melody and harmony, the piano occupies a unique position in the history of music, serving as a solo instrument, a compositional tool, and an accompaniment in virtually every genre.

The piano evolved from earlier stringed keyboard instruments such as the **harpsichord** and **clavichord**, but it was Italian inventor **Bartolomeo Cristofori**, around 1700, who made the critical breakthrough: replacing the plucking mechanism of the harpsichord with hammers that struck the strings. This innovation gave rise to the name "pianoforte" (literally, "soft-loud"), because it allowed dynamic control through touch—a revolutionary feature at the time.

Throughout the 18th and 19th centuries, the piano underwent rapid refinement. Builders developed stronger frames, expanded the range of keys, and introduced innovations such as the **sustain pedal**, enabling longer resonance and greater expressive control. These improvements paralleled the rise of piano-centric composition. Composers like **Beethoven, Chopin, Liszt,** and **Debussy** wrote music that not only showcased the piano's expanding capabilities but also elevated it to a central role in Western music.

The piano also became a cultural fixture in middle- and upper-class households across Europe and the Americas, symbolizing education, refinement, and social aspiration. In the parlors and salons of the 19th century, the piano was a social tool as much as a musical one—a gathering point for music-making, courtship, and expression.

Beyond its classical roots, the piano made vital contributions to 20th-century music, particularly in **jazz**, **blues**, and **popular music**. Artists like **Duke Ellington**, **Thelonious Monk**, and **Ray Charles** harnessed its percussive and harmonic versatility to forge new genres, while pianists like **Nina Simone** and **Elton John** brought emotional depth and storytelling to the instrument in contemporary music.

Whether in the concert hall, the jazz club, or the recording studio, the piano remains unparalleled in its range and adaptability. It serves as the backbone for music education and a gateway to composition, providing the structural canvas upon which musical ideas take shape. Its evolution mirrors the development of Western music itself—rich, complex, and continuously reinvented.

The Electric Guitar: Voice of a Generation

If the Stradivarius violin speaks to tradition and the piano to versatility, the **electric guitar** roars with the energy of revolution. Introduced in the 1930s and perfected over subsequent decades, the electric guitar transformed not only how music was played but what music could represent. More than an instrument, it became an emblem of youthful rebellion, countercultural identity, and sonic exploration.

Early pioneers such as **Les Paul**, who invented the solid-body electric guitar, and **Leo Fender**, whose Stratocaster and Telecaster models became icons, revolutionized music-making. These innovations removed the limitations of acoustic resonance, allowing musicians to amplify, distort, and manipulate sound in unprecedented ways. Paired with the evolution of the **amplifier** and the **effects pedal**, the electric guitar opened new worlds of expression.

In the hands of artists like **Jimi Hendrix**, **Eric Clapton**, **Jimmy Page**, and later **Eddie Van Halen**, the electric guitar became a conduit for unfiltered emotion and technical wizardry. Hendrix's groundbreaking use of feedback and distortion at Woodstock, for example, symbolized both musical innovation and political defiance. Rock music, fueled by electric guitar riffs and solos, became the soundtrack of social movements, from anti-war protests to civil rights campaigns.

The instrument's cultural reach extended far beyond rock. In **blues**, it electrified the raw emotion of artists like **Muddy Waters** and **B.B. King**. In **jazz**, guitarists such as **Wes Montgomery** and **Pat Metheny** expanded the instrument's harmonic vocabulary. Even in modern **pop**, **hip-hop**, and **electronic** music, the electric guitar retains a presence, whether sampled, looped, or synthesized.

But what sets the electric guitar apart isn't just its sound; it's its symbolism. It represents the democratization of music. Inexpensive, portable, and accessible, it invited millions of young people to pick up an instrument and express themselves. Unlike the exclusivity associated with classical instruments, the electric guitar was the people's instrument—a tool for self-definition and collective identity.

Moreover, its aesthetic—shaped by sleek designs, vivid colors, and wild stage antics—turned musicians into icons. The electric guitar was as visual as it was auditory, contributing to the rise of the rock star and changing how performance itself was understood.

5.2 Musical Works Defining Eras

Throughout history, certain musical compositions and performances have not only captivated audiences but also defined entire eras. These works often transcend their immediate musical value, becoming cultural landmarks that encapsulate the sentiments, aspirations, and challenges of their time. From orchestral masterpieces that redefined the boundaries of classical form, to groundbreaking albums that transformed popular music, these milestones illustrate the unique ability of music to reflect and shape the human experience.

One of the most enduring musical works in Western history is **Ludwig van Beethoven's Ninth Symphony**, completed in 1824. Often hailed as one of the greatest achievements in classical music, the Ninth Symphony marked a dramatic departure from traditional symphonic structure and introduced revolutionary elements that would influence composers for generations. It was the first major symphony to include **vocals and a full chorus**, incorporating Friedrich Schiller's "Ode to Joy" as a rousing finale—a powerful anthem of unity and universal brotherhood.

Beethoven's Ninth stands as a monumental bridge between the Classical and Romantic periods. Its scale, emotional depth, and complexity surpassed all previous symphonic efforts. What makes this piece particularly extraordinary is that it was composed while Beethoven was **completely deaf**—a staggering testament to his genius and resilience. The symphony's final movement, with its triumphant and inclusive choral affirmation, has become a universal symbol of humanistic ideals. It has been performed at significant moments in history—from the fall of the Berlin Wall to the Olympic Games—serving as a sonic banner of hope, peace, and perseverance.

If Beethoven's Ninth was a defining moment of 19th-century Western music, the **Jazz Age** of the early 20th century represented an entirely different kind of cultural revolution. At the heart of this movement was **Louis Armstrong**, a trumpet virtuoso, innovative vocalist, and charismatic performer who helped bring jazz into the American mainstream and beyond. Born in New Orleans in 1901, Armstrong emerged from humble beginnings to become one of the most influential figures in American music.

Armstrong's contributions to jazz cannot be overstated. He redefined the role of the soloist in ensemble settings, transforming jazz from a collective group improvisation into a platform for individual expression. His recordings with the **Hot Five and Hot Seven**, including classics like "West End Blues" and "Potato Head Blues," showcased not only his technical mastery but also his unparalleled ability to convey emotion and swing through phrasing and rhythm.

Beyond technical prowess, Armstrong introduced a deeply human voice into jazz, both literally and figuratively. His distinctive gravelly tone, playful scatting, and infectious charisma helped jazz gain wider acceptance, influencing artists from Ella Fitzgerald to Miles Davis. During a time of intense racial segregation, Armstrong's talent and popularity also made him an unofficial ambassador for Black American culture. His music became a form of resistance, celebration, and cultural pride, playing a key role in the development of modern music around the world.

Moving forward to the mid-20th century, another musical revolution was brewing across the Atlantic: **The Beatles**. Rising from the industrial city of Liverpool in the early 1960s, The Beatles—**John Lennon, Paul McCartney, George Harrison, and Ringo Starr**—quickly became global icons, fundamentally altering the trajectory of popular music and ushering in a new era of artistic experimentation.

What began as catchy rock 'n' roll tunes with "She Loves You" and "I Want to Hold Your Hand" evolved into a sophisticated musical journey marked by innovation and introspection. Albums like **"Revolver"**, **"Sgt. Pepper's Lonely**

Hearts Club Band"**, and **"The White Album"** pushed the boundaries of recording techniques, instrumentation, and lyrical themes. The Beatles were among the first mainstream artists to experiment with **multi-track recording, psychedelic effects, Indian instruments**, and **classical orchestration**—elements that had rarely, if ever, been merged into the pop format.

Their music reflected the rapidly changing cultural landscape of the 1960s, engaging with topics ranging from love and self-discovery to war, drug use, and spiritual exploration. As artists, they encouraged listeners to expand their sonic horizons and question societal norms. As a cultural force, they helped define the spirit of a generation seeking liberation, authenticity, and connection.

The Beatles' influence went beyond music: their evolving style, public statements, and even hairstyles became symbols of youth identity and countercultural rebellion. Few bands have managed to maintain both commercial appeal and artistic integrity on such a massive scale. To this day, their albums remain cultural touchstones, continuously rediscovered by new generations who find in them a reflection of both personal and collective journeys.

Together, **Beethoven's Ninth Symphony, Louis Armstrong's jazz legacy**, and **The Beatles' groundbreaking albums** represent more than musical milestones—they are **sonic monuments** to the eras they shaped. Each speaks to a different dimension of the human condition: the philosophical quest for meaning, the improvisational joy of freedom, and the artistic rebellion of innovation. Their enduring relevance is proof that music, in its highest form, is not just entertainment—it is a chronicle of civilization.

5.3 The Cultural Impact of Rhythm

Rhythm—the heartbeat of music—is one of the most ancient and elemental forms of human expression. Long before language was formalized into writing or melodies captured on sheet music, rhythm was used to communicate, celebrate, mourn, and connect. Around the world, rhythmic traditions have not only shaped musical genres but also defined cultural identities, inspired resistance movements, and given voice to the voiceless. Among the most impactful rhythmic legacies are **African drum traditions, Samba and Tango**, and the **rise of Hip-Hop**—each rooted in specific histories yet resonant across global soundscapes.

In many ways, the **drum** is the original musical instrument, and nowhere is its cultural importance more deeply felt than in **sub-Saharan Africa**. African drum traditions have long served as a means of **communication**, **ritual**, and **community cohesion**. More than musical instruments, drums such as the **djembe**, **talking drum**, and **dundun** are considered sacred tools, often used in ceremonies marking birth, initiation, marriage, and death.

Each drumbeat carries meaning—both musically and symbolically. Drummers are often storytellers, historians, and spiritual leaders within their communities. The polyrhythmic structures typical of African music—where multiple rhythms interlock and respond to each other—mirror communal values of **interdependence and dialogue**. These complex rhythms require deep listening and synchronization, reinforcing social harmony and shared identity.

African drumming traditions profoundly influenced global music through the transatlantic slave trade, where enslaved Africans brought their rhythms to the Americas and the Caribbean. These rhythms laid the **foundation for countless genres**, including blues, jazz, reggae, salsa, samba, and hip-hop. The survival and adaptation of African rhythms amid cultural erasure and diaspora resistance remain one of the most powerful examples of cultural resilience through sound.

Two of the most rhythmically rich and culturally expressive musical forms to emerge from this lineage are **Samba** and **Tango**—each a vibrant fusion of African, European, and Indigenous influences that rose to prominence in **Brazil** and **Argentina**, respectively.

Samba, born in the Afro-Brazilian communities of Rio de Janeiro, is a celebration of life, struggle, and identity. Its infectious rhythms—characterized by syncopation, call-and-response, and layered percussion—are the lifeblood of **Carnival**, Brazil's most famous cultural festival. Instruments such as the **surdo**, **tamborim**, and **cuíca** create a pulsing groove that drives the dance and connects generations of performers and revelers.

More than festive music, Samba has been a **symbol of resistance**. In its early days, it was marginalized and criminalized by Brazilian authorities due to its association with Black culture and the poor. Yet it persisted, gradually gaining acceptance and eventually becoming a national symbol. Today, Samba schools not only preserve musical traditions but also provide education, community support, and a platform for social commentary.

Tango, emerging from the port neighborhoods of Buenos Aires in the late 19th century, tells a different but equally rich story. Born from a mixture of African rhythms, Spanish melodies, and Italian immigration, Tango combines dramatic syncopation with melancholic melodies, often centered around themes of longing, exile, and urban life.

Performed with instruments like the **bandoneón, violin**, and **piano**, Tango music mirrors the sensuality and intensity of its dance counterpart. It gained global fame in the early 20th century and became a vehicle for Argentine national identity. Like Samba, Tango began in marginalized spaces—bordellos, taverns, immigrant enclaves—and climbed to international stages and elite salons. Its rise embodies music's power to transform social stigma into cultural prestige.

In the late 20th century, a new rhythmic revolution took shape in the **urban neighborhoods of the Bronx**: the birth of **Hip-Hop**. Emerging in the 1970s among African American and Latino youth, Hip-Hop began as a grassroots movement encompassing **DJing, MCing (rapping), breakdancing, and graffiti art**. Central to its identity was rhythm—whether the looped breakbeats of DJs like **Kool Herc** or the poetic cadence of early MCs.

What began as block party entertainment soon evolved into a powerful cultural force. **Hip-Hop gave voice to marginalized communities**, addressing systemic racism, police brutality, economic inequality, and urban resilience. Tracks like **"The Message"** by Grandmaster Flash and the Furious Five, **Public Enemy's** political anthems, and later **Tupac Shakur's** lyrical meditations spoke to generations of listeners seeking truth and solidarity.

The genre's rhythm-driven style—defined by beats, flow, and lyrical dexterity—proved incredibly adaptable. By the 1990s and 2000s, Hip-Hop had gone global, inspiring localized movements in France, South Africa, Japan, and beyond. It became not just a musical genre but a **cultural movement**, shaping fashion, language, politics, and media.

Hip-Hop's rhythmic innovation continues today, blending with other genres like R&B, electronic, and Afrobeat. Artists such as **Kendrick Lamar, Missy Elliott**, and **J. Cole** use rhythm to tell complex stories, challenge social norms, and redefine what music—and art—can achieve.

Chapter 6: Science's Game-Changers

"The important thing is to never stop questioning." — Albert Einstein

6.1 Groundbreaking Discoveries

Science has long stood as one of humanity's most profound endeavors—an evolving method of inquiry aimed at understanding the world through observation, evidence, and reason. At its best, science does more than explain phenomena; it redefines our place within the universe. Throughout history, there have been moments when a single work, insight, or experiment shifted the entire framework of knowledge. These scientific breakthroughs became inflection points—altering not only how we see the natural world but also how we organize society, perceive life, and understand ourselves.

Among the most transformative scientific achievements in human history are **Isaac Newton's** *Philosophiæ Naturalis Principia Mathematica*, **Charles Darwin's** *On the Origin of Species*, and the **discovery of DNA's structure**. Each of these discoveries fundamentally reshaped our intellectual landscape. Together, they form a triumvirate of scientific revolution—explaining the motion of planets, the development of life, and the very building blocks of heredity. They did not merely answer questions; they raised new ones, inspiring generations of thinkers and innovators to explore further.

Isaac Newton's *Principia Mathematica* – The Clockwork Universe

In 1687, English physicist and mathematician **Isaac Newton** published a treatise that would become one of the most significant works in the history of science: *Philosophiæ Naturalis Principia Mathematica*, often referred to simply as the *Principia*. With it, Newton unified celestial and terrestrial mechanics under one grand theory of motion, offering for the first time a set of universal laws that applied both to the heavens and the Earth.

The *Principia* laid out **Newton's three laws of motion**—principles that became the foundation of classical mechanics. It also introduced the **law of universal**

gravitation, the idea that every mass attracts every other mass in the universe with a force directly proportional to the product of their masses and inversely proportional to the square of the distance between them. This was nothing short of revolutionary. For the first time, a single mathematical formula could explain both the fall of an apple and the orbit of the moon.

Newton's work was not created in a vacuum. He stood on the shoulders of previous giants, including **Galileo Galilei, Johannes Kepler**, and **René Descartes**. However, it was Newton who synthesized their insights into a coherent framework, using the newly developed tools of **calculus** (which he co-invented) and geometric reasoning. His mathematical rigor allowed scientists to predict the motion of objects with unprecedented accuracy, ushering in what became known as the **Age of Enlightenment**—a period where reason and empirical science began to challenge religious dogma and superstition.

The broader cultural impact of *Principia* was immense. Newton's universe was one of order and predictability—a **mechanical cosmos** governed by laws that could be understood and manipulated. This vision had profound philosophical implications. It suggested that nature could be tamed, understood, and improved through rational inquiry. Governments, economies, and societies began to value empirical evidence and objective knowledge, laying the groundwork for modern scientific institutions and technological progress.

Though later developments, particularly Einstein's theory of relativity and quantum mechanics, would reveal the limitations of Newtonian physics at extreme scales, Newton's principles remain deeply embedded in engineering, architecture, and everyday science. The *Principia* remains a testament to the power of mathematics in unlocking the secrets of the cosmos.

Charles Darwin's *On the Origin of Species* – Evolution as a Unifying Theory

Nearly two centuries after Newton, another Englishman would publish a book that would forever alter humanity's understanding of life itself. In 1859, **Charles Darwin** released *On the Origin of Species by Means of Natural Selection*, a work that would come to be considered the foundational text of **evolutionary biology**.

In this meticulously argued volume, Darwin proposed that all species of life have descended over time from common ancestors. The mechanism driving this change, he argued, was **natural selection**—a process by which heritable traits that increase an organism's chance of survival and reproduction become more common in successive generations. With this elegant explanation, Darwin provided a unifying theory for the diversity of life on Earth.

The implications of Darwin's theory were as profound as they were controversial. It challenged traditional views of creation, contradicting the prevailing belief that species were fixed and individually created. More provocatively, it placed **human beings within the continuum of the natural world**, suggesting that Homo sapiens shared common ancestry with other animals—a notion that rattled religious and philosophical assumptions about human uniqueness.

Darwin was not the first to propose evolutionary ideas—figures like **Jean-Baptiste Lamarck** had suggested similar concepts earlier—but Darwin's theory was distinguished by its vast empirical evidence and rigorous logic. He had spent years gathering data, most notably during his voyage on the HMS Beagle, where his observations in the Galápagos Islands helped formulate his theories. The breadth of his evidence—from fossils and geographic distribution to embryology and morphology—offered compelling support for his revolutionary ideas.

The publication of *Origin of Species* ignited fierce debate, both scientific and cultural. Over time, as genetics and molecular biology advanced, Darwin's ideas gained increasing support, eventually forming the bedrock of modern biology. The **Neo-Darwinian synthesis**, combining Mendelian genetics with natural selection, provided a more robust framework for understanding evolution and heredity.

Darwin's work did more than revolutionize biology—it transformed how humans saw themselves in relation to nature. Evolution provided a framework for understanding human origins, behavior, and even culture, influencing fields from psychology and anthropology to sociology and ethics. It redefined questions about life's purpose and place, forcing humanity to reckon with a new kind of humility: we were not the apex of creation, but one branch on a vast, interconnected tree of life.

The Discovery of DNA – The Code of Life

If Newton revealed the rules of motion and Darwin explained the diversity of life, the 20th century brought another transformative breakthrough: the discovery of **DNA's double-helix structure**, which unveiled the molecular basis of heredity. This discovery didn't just explain how traits were passed from generation to generation—it unlocked the language of life itself.

In 1953, **James Watson** and **Francis Crick**, working at the University of Cambridge, proposed a now-iconic model of **deoxyribonucleic acid (DNA)** as a **double helix**, with two intertwined strands composed of nucleotide bases—adenine, thymine, cytosine, and guanine—held together by hydrogen bonds. The model explained how genetic information could be **copied and transmitted**, revealing a mechanism for heredity at the molecular level.

Their discovery was based on critical work by other scientists, including **Rosalind Franklin**, whose X-ray crystallography images were instrumental in identifying the helical structure. Her contributions, though underappreciated at the time, are now recognized as vital to one of the greatest scientific achievements of the 20th century.

Understanding DNA's structure revolutionized biology and medicine. It provided answers to long-standing questions about inheritance, mutation, and genetic disorders. It led to the development of **genetic engineering**, **DNA fingerprinting**, and eventually the **Human Genome Project**, which mapped the entire human genetic code.

The social and ethical implications were just as significant. The ability to manipulate DNA opened the door to **gene therapy**, **genetically modified organisms (GMOs)**, and **personalized medicine**, while also raising complex questions about privacy, ethics, and the definition of life. DNA evidence transformed criminal justice systems, paternity testing, and ancestry tracing, turning once-inaccessible scientific ideas into everyday tools.

On a philosophical level, the discovery of DNA forced a reconceptualization of identity. It demonstrated that all life shares a common biochemical foundation—that the genetic code is universal among living organisms. It reminded humanity, once again, that our distinctions are less significant than our shared origins, deepening the evolutionary insights Darwin had laid out a century earlier.

6.2 Inventions that Altered the Course of History

Science is often associated with discovery, but equally transformative is the application of that knowledge through invention. Throughout human history, certain tools and machines have not merely improved life—they have fundamentally changed the trajectory of civilization. These inventions were not confined to the laboratories in which they emerged; they reshaped economies, redefined human potential, and transformed how we perceive reality itself. Among the most impactful are the **telescope and microscope**, the **steam engine**, and the **computer**—each unlocking new dimensions of understanding and sparking revolutions that continue to influence our world.

The **telescope**, first developed in the early 17th century, revolutionized humanity's understanding of the cosmos. Though **Hans Lippershey** is often credited with creating the first working version, it was **Galileo Galilei** who used the instrument to turn the heavens into a realm of empirical inquiry. With his improvements to magnification, Galileo observed the moons of Jupiter, the phases of Venus, sunspots, and the rugged terrain of the Moon. These observations contradicted the long-standing geocentric model of the universe, which had placed Earth at its center, and lent strong support to **Copernicus' heliocentric theory**.

The cultural implications were enormous. The telescope, in essence, challenged centuries of theological and philosophical dogma. It displaced humanity from the presumed center of the universe and catalyzed the **Scientific Revolution**, a movement that emphasized observation and evidence over inherited authority. Galileo's conflict with the Catholic Church underscored the friction between emerging science and established power structures—a tension that still echoes today.

At the opposite end of the scale, the **microscope** opened a new world inward. First refined by **Antonie van Leeuwenhoek** and **Robert Hooke**, the microscope allowed scientists to peer into the intricacies of biological life. Hooke's *Micrographia* in 1665 introduced the term "cell" after he observed the cellular structure of cork. Leeuwenhoek's observations of "animalcules" in pond water revealed an invisible universe teeming with life.

The microscope sparked foundational advances in **medicine, microbiology, and genetics**. It laid the groundwork for understanding disease, reproduction, and the building blocks of living organisms. It brought us closer to answering fundamental questions about what it means to be alive. Just as the telescope expanded our grasp of the cosmos, the microscope shrank the world down to its smallest yet most essential parts, revealing that the laws of nature operate with astonishing complexity and elegance at every scale.

If the telescope and microscope expanded the horizons of thought, the **steam engine** transformed the practical realities of human existence. Its invention was not the product of a single mind but a series of innovations refined over time, particularly by **James Watt** in the late 18th century. Watt's improvements, including the separate condenser, made steam power more efficient and applicable across industries.

The steam engine fueled the **Industrial Revolution**, a seismic shift in global history. For the first time, human labor and animal power were no longer the primary engines of productivity. Factories, mills, and transport systems became mechanized, leading to massive increases in production and profound social change. Urbanization accelerated as people moved to cities for work, and entirely new industries emerged, altering patterns of wealth, class, and labor.

Steam-powered trains and ships shrank distances, enabling faster trade and travel. The engine helped turn local economies into **global networks**. However, it also brought environmental and social challenges—child labor, pollution, and exploitation—that forced societies to grapple with the costs of progress. In every sense, the steam engine was more than a machine; it was the harbinger of a new era of human capability and complexity.

In the 20th century, another invention would redefine human capacity yet again: the **computer**. Unlike previous tools, which augmented physical abilities, the computer amplified **cognitive power**. Early mechanical computers like **Charles Babbage's Analytical Engine** hinted at this potential, but it was in the mid-20th century—with figures like **Alan Turing**, **John von Neumann**, and **Grace Hopper**—that electronic computers became a reality.

Computers began as tools for complex calculations, particularly in wartime contexts such as codebreaking and ballistic trajectory modeling. But their evolution into **programmable, general-purpose machines** set the stage for the digital age. The invention of the **microprocessor** in the 1970s shrank machines from room-sized giants to devices that could fit on a desk—and later, in a pocket.

The impact of computing is incalculable. Computers now permeate every aspect of life: communication, finance, education, medicine, entertainment, and beyond. The rise of **artificial intelligence**, **machine learning**, and **cloud computing** has redefined what machines can do and what it means to be intelligent. Entire economies are now built on information rather than industry, and society has been reshaped around data flows and algorithms.

Computers have also democratized knowledge, giving unprecedented access to information. But they have introduced new vulnerabilities—cybersecurity threats, digital divides, and ethical dilemmas surrounding surveillance and autonomy. Like the telescope, microscope, and steam engine before them, computers changed not only what we could do, but how we think about our place in the world.

6.3 Science as a Cultural Catalyst

Scientific progress does more than expand the boundaries of knowledge—it reshapes how societies see themselves. At pivotal moments in history, science has acted as a **cultural catalyst**, challenging assumptions, redefining identities, and sparking new forms of collective imagination. The artifacts and milestones that exemplify this role—such as the **Moon landing, CERN's Large Hadron Collider**, and the development of **vaccines and antibiotics**—reflect the deep entanglement of science with philosophy, politics, and culture.

On **July 20, 1969**, humans set foot on the Moon for the first time. The **Apollo 11 mission**, led by **Neil Armstrong**, **Buzz Aldrin**, and **Michael Collins**, was not merely a technological triumph—it was a moment of collective awe. When Armstrong declared, "That's one small step for man, one giant leap for mankind," he articulated more than a personal achievement. He spoke to humanity's desire to transcend its limitations.

The Moon landing was the culmination of decades of scientific innovation, driven in part by Cold War rivalries between the United States and the Soviet Union. But it became something greater—a shared vision of what humanity could achieve when knowledge, ambition, and cooperation aligned. The images of Earth from space, captured during these missions, gave birth to a **global consciousness**. For the first time, people could see their planet as a fragile sphere in a vast cosmos, fueling environmental awareness and a sense of planetary unity.

Artifacts from the Moon landing—lunar rocks, space suits, the iconic footprint in lunar dust—are now preserved in museums, serving as symbols of possibility.

They remind us that science is not abstract; it is capable of transforming imagination into reality.

A more recent scientific marvel, the **Large Hadron Collider (LHC)** at **CERN**, continues this legacy of pushing boundaries. Located beneath the Franco-Swiss border, the LHC is the world's largest and most powerful particle accelerator. Completed in 2008, it allows physicists to recreate the conditions that existed fractions of a second after the Big Bang.

In 2012, the LHC enabled the discovery of the **Higgs boson**, a particle long theorized but never before observed. Its detection confirmed the **Standard Model** of particle physics and offered deeper insight into how matter acquires mass. This discovery was not just a victory for physics—it was a cultural moment, celebrated across the globe as a triumph of collective human intellect.

CERN itself is a unique institution, employing thousands of scientists from over 100 countries. It operates as a beacon of international collaboration, proving that shared scientific goals can transcend borders and politics. In a world often divided by ideology, the LHC demonstrates that curiosity and cooperation remain potent unifiers.

While physics probes the fabric of the universe, **medicine**—especially through **vaccines** and **antibiotics**—has reshaped the conditions of human life on Earth. The development of vaccines, beginning with **Edward Jenner's smallpox vaccine** in the 18th century, inaugurated a new era in public health. By exposing the body to weakened or inactive pathogens, vaccines stimulate immunity, protecting individuals and communities from deadly diseases.

Vaccines have **eradicated smallpox**, nearly eliminated **polio**, and drastically reduced mortality from illnesses like **measles**, **tetanus**, and **influenza**. Their impact on child survival, lifespan, and global development is unparalleled. Vaccination campaigns have become symbols of solidarity and scientific progress, though they also remind us of the challenges of misinformation and access.

Antibiotics, first discovered by **Alexander Fleming** in 1928 with the accidental identification of **penicillin**, revolutionized the treatment of bacterial infections. Before antibiotics, even minor wounds or routine surgeries carried deadly risks. The ability to target and eliminate bacteria without harming the host transformed medicine, allowing for safer childbirth, transplants, and cancer therapies.

Yet, the rise of **antibiotic resistance** underscores the ongoing relationship between science and responsibility. These life-saving tools require stewardship and equitable distribution, especially as global disparities in healthcare persist.

Together, vaccines and antibiotics exemplify science as a **force for liberation**—freeing humanity from the grip of disease and redefining our potential. They reflect science's most humanitarian impulse: to preserve and enhance life.

6.4 Scientific Instruments and Devices

Throughout history, humankind has gazed into the unknown and sought to understand it—not only with wonder but with tools. While the ancients crafted myths to explain the movements of stars or the mechanics of nature, it was the scientific instrument that shifted the paradigm. These tools allowed us not just to speculate, but to measure, observe, and prove. They extended our senses, challenged assumptions, and altered the way we perceived the universe and our place within it.

This chapter is a celebration of three transformative instruments that symbolize key turning points in scientific history: Galileo's telescope, the ancient and intricate astrolabe, and Newton's reflecting mirror. Each of these devices—distinct in form and separated by centuries—helped shift humanity's understanding of the cosmos from guesswork to precision. They were not mere gadgets; they were lenses through which the universe revealed itself, slowly and often reluctantly.

Galileo's Telescope: A New View of the Heavens

In 1609, a middle-aged Italian mathematician and professor of mechanics turned a simple spyglass toward the sky—and changed the course of history. The man was Galileo Galilei, and the device he held was a telescope of his own making, based on designs that had only recently emerged in the Netherlands. Though the basic principle was not his invention, what Galileo did with it was revolutionary.

Before Galileo, the heavens were considered immutable and perfect—a realm of divine order. This belief, inherited from Aristotle and refined through centuries of theological dogma, held that celestial bodies were smooth, flawless, and eternal. But when Galileo pointed his improved telescope—magnifying around 20 times—at the moon, he didn't see divine perfection. He saw **craters**, **mountains**, and **shadows**. The moon, it turned out, was not unlike Earth.

From there, his observations only grew more unsettling to the established worldview. He discovered **four moons orbiting Jupiter**—now known as the Galilean moons—proving that not everything revolved around the Earth. He observed the **phases of Venus**, which could only be explained if Venus orbited the sun, not the Earth. He noted **sunspots** on the surface of the sun, contradicting the notion of heavenly incorruptibility.

Galileo's telescope was, physically, a simple refracting instrument. It used a convex objective lens and a concave eyepiece to magnify distant objects. But it was also, metaphorically, a weapon. With it, Galileo assaulted the Ptolemaic model of the cosmos and gave powerful support to the Copernican system, which placed the sun—not Earth—at the center of the solar system.

The backlash was swift. The Church, uneasy with the implications of a heliocentric universe, condemned Galileo's findings. In 1633, he was tried for heresy and forced to recant. Yet the damage to the old worldview was done. The telescope had opened a door that could no longer be closed.

Galileo's instrument survives today in Florence, and it is shockingly modest in appearance. A tube of wood and brass, smaller than a walking stick, yet powerful enough to fracture a millennium of celestial certainty. It reminds us that sometimes, all it takes to rewrite the universe is to look through a new lens.

Astrolabes: The Ancient Calculators of the Sky

Long before Galileo tilted a telescope skyward, ancient scientists and navigators looked to the heavens with a different instrument in hand: the **astrolabe**. Revered as one of the most elegant and versatile scientific tools of antiquity and the medieval world, the astrolabe was a portable model of the cosmos, an analog computer of astonishing complexity and grace.

The origins of the astrolabe are difficult to trace precisely. Hellenistic astronomers, such as Hipparchus and Ptolemy, laid the mathematical groundwork for its development, but it was in the Islamic Golden Age—between the 8th and 14th centuries—that the astrolabe reached its full flowering. Islamic scholars in cities like Baghdad, Córdoba, and Cairo perfected the design, adding innovations and inscriptions that blended science, art, and spirituality.

At its core, the astrolabe is based on **stereographic projection**, a method of projecting the three-dimensional sky onto a two-dimensional plane. The instrument typically consists of a circular base plate (called the *mater*), which holds a number of interchangeable plates (*tympans*) engraved with coordinate lines specific to different latitudes. Over this sits a rotating component called the *rete*, which resembles a delicate skeleton map of the stars. A rule or sighting device—known as an *alidade*—allows the user to align the device with celestial bodies.

What could the astrolabe do? Quite a lot. It could **determine the time of day or night**, **locate the positions of stars and planets**, **find the altitude of celestial bodies**, **calculate prayer times and the direction of Mecca**, and even aid in **navigation and surveying**. For centuries, it was the scientific instrument par excellence, bridging disciplines from astronomy and mathematics to theology and cartography.

But the astrolabe was more than a technical device. It was a **symbol of cosmological order**—a physical representation of the interconnectedness of Earth and sky. Many were beautifully crafted from brass or bronze, engraved with calligraphy, astrological signs, and poetic verses. Possessing an astrolabe was a mark of intellectual sophistication, and they were prized gifts among scholars and rulers alike.

Perhaps what's most astonishing is the **durability of the design**. Astrolabes were used continuously for over a thousand years, with little fundamental change. Even as mechanical clocks and telescopes emerged, the astrolabe remained in use for its reliability and versatility. Some versions were tailored for specific cities; others were "universal" models capable of adapting to different latitudes—a testament to the scientific ambition of their makers.

In a world before satellites and smartphones, the astrolabe was a portable universe—elegant, exacting, and endlessly revealing.

Newton's Reflecting Mirror: Revolution Through Reflection

While Galileo brought the heavens closer, it was **Isaac Newton** who brought clarity to the tools themselves. In the late 17th century, Newton revolutionized telescope design by addressing a fundamental flaw in refracting telescopes like Galileo's: **chromatic aberration**. This distortion, caused by the bending of light through lenses, produced fringes of color around observed objects, limiting the clarity and size of magnified images.

Newton's solution was as elegant as it was transformative. Instead of bending light through glass lenses, he proposed **reflecting it using mirrors**. In 1668, he built the first practical **reflecting telescope**, a design that would forever change astronomy.

The Newtonian telescope used a **concave primary mirror** to gather and focus light, and a **flat diagonal secondary mirror** to reflect that light sideways into an eyepiece. This approach eliminated chromatic aberration entirely and allowed for a shorter, more compact telescope with a wider field of view. It also opened the door for much larger telescopes, as mirrors could be made bigger and sturdier than lenses without sacrificing optical quality.

Newton's own telescope was modest in scale—about six inches long—but it proved the concept. With it, he could clearly observe the moons of Jupiter, the phases of Venus, and the rings of Saturn. But perhaps more importantly, his invention sparked a wave of innovation. Later telescopes built on Newton's design would unlock the secrets of distant galaxies, nebulae, and the expanding universe itself.

The significance of Newton's telescope wasn't just in what it could see—it was in **how** it saw. It demonstrated the power of applied physics and precision engineering. It showed that by understanding the behavior of light, we could build instruments that weren't limited by the human eye, or even by the materials of traditional optics.

Newton's reflecting mirror wasn't an isolated invention; it was part of a broader **scientific revolution**. Alongside his laws of motion and universal gravitation, the telescope was one more proof that the universe was not governed by caprice or mystery, but by **principles**—knowable, observable, and, with the right tools, testable.

Today, virtually all large astronomical telescopes—from the Hale Telescope at Palomar to the James Webb Space Telescope—owe their lineage to Newton's mirror. His design endures not only in astronomy but also in modern physics, where the principle of reflection continues to play a role in optical instruments, laser systems, and beyond.

The Instruments That Changed Our Minds

What unites these three devices—Galileo's telescope, the astrolabe, and Newton's reflecting mirror—is not just their scientific importance but their **philosophical impact**. Each, in its own way, redefined how we understand the universe and ourselves.

The telescope shattered the illusion of Earth's centrality. The astrolabe harmonized mathematical complexity with spiritual need, blending the rational and the divine. The reflecting mirror, humble in form, was a key that unlocked the stars with unprecedented clarity. They are reminders that the act of seeing is never passive. It is shaped by the instruments we build, the questions we ask, and the courage we have to challenge what we thought we knew.

These are not merely artifacts of science—they are artifacts of **curiosity**, of **daring**, of the unshakable human impulse to understand. They sit at the intersection of art, mathematics, craftsmanship, and philosophy. They are proof that tools can be beautiful, and beauty can be precise.

Centuries later, we still gaze upward, still ask questions, still build machines to sharpen our view. But the foundations were laid long ago—in wood and brass, in carved plates and curved mirrors, by minds who dared to look differently.

Chapter 7: Engineering Wonders and Human Ingenuity

"Scientists dream about doing great things. Engineers do them." — James A. Michener

7.1 Structures that Defied Limits

Throughout history, the boundaries of what is physically possible have been repeatedly redrawn by the hands of engineers. While science often begins with theory, engineering turns ideas into tangible form—concrete, steel, earth, and water manipulated into systems and structures that serve civilization. Some engineering feats, by virtue of their scale, complexity, and ambition, have done more than meet functional needs—they have reshaped the map, mastered nature's force, and redefined human capability. In this chapter, we explore three such monumental achievements: the **Panama and Suez Canals**, the **Hoover Dam**, and the **skyscraper**. Each one stands not only as a marvel of its time but also as a lasting symbol of human ingenuity, perseverance, and the desire to shape our world.

The Panama and Suez Canals: Rewriting the Map

Few engineering projects in history have so literally redrawn the global landscape as the **Panama Canal** and the **Suez Canal**. These two waterway megaprojects severed continents and connected oceans, collapsing the barriers of geography and revolutionizing global trade.

The **Suez Canal**, located in northeastern Egypt, connects the Mediterranean Sea to the Red Sea, linking Europe to Asia without the need to circumnavigate the entire African continent. Proposed in various forms since antiquity, it wasn't until the 19th century that technology and geopolitics aligned to make it a reality. Under the leadership of French diplomat **Ferdinand de Lesseps**, construction began in 1859 and took ten years to complete. When it officially opened in 1869, the Suez Canal stretched over 160 kilometers through desert sands—an unprecedented linear excavation project at the time.

Unlike the Panama Canal, the Suez is a **sea-level canal**, meaning it requires no locks or lifts. This simplicity belies the monumental effort involved in its construction, especially given the harsh working conditions and the rudimentary machinery available at the time. Tens of thousands of laborers, many of them conscripted, toiled under the Egyptian sun with picks and shovels, facing heat, disease, and exhaustion.

The economic impact of the Suez Canal was immediate and profound. Shipping distances between Europe and Asia were reduced by over 7,000 kilometers, dramatically lowering transportation costs and expanding trade routes. The canal also became a critical geopolitical asset, controlling access between East and West—a significance that continues today, as seen in global economic disruptions during its rare closures.

Less than 50 years later, on the opposite side of the world, another audacious vision was coming to life: the **Panama Canal**. Stretching approximately 80 kilometers across the Isthmus of Panama, this canal would allow ships to pass between the Atlantic and Pacific Oceans without making the perilous journey around Cape Horn at the southern tip of South America.

The first attempt to build the canal was also led by Ferdinand de Lesseps, fresh off his success in Egypt. But the dense jungles, mountainous terrain, and devastating tropical diseases of Panama proved too much. The French effort collapsed in the 1880s, bankrupting investors and costing over 20,000 lives.

The project was revived by the United States in 1904, under the leadership of **President Theodore Roosevelt**, and completed in 1914. This iteration required entirely new engineering strategies, including the construction of a **lock system** to raise and lower ships across the elevation of the isthmus. The centerpiece of the project was the **Gatun Dam and Lake**, which created an artificial body of water to help facilitate passage and manage seasonal floods.

The construction of the Panama Canal was a landmark in engineering, medical science, and logistics. American engineers brought in steam shovels, railroads, and massive dredgers. Simultaneously, public health officials led by **Dr. William Gorgas** implemented one of the first large-scale mosquito eradication campaigns to combat malaria and yellow fever, significantly reducing mortality and proving that infrastructure and public health are inseparable.

Today, both canals are essential arteries of international commerce. They symbolize the human will to bend geography to our needs and remain some of the most heavily trafficked and strategically important transit routes in the world. They are testaments to how engineering can change not just landscapes but the entire flow of global civilization.

The Hoover Dam: Harnessing a River, Building a Region

If the canals represent our effort to traverse the globe, the **Hoover Dam** represents humanity's effort to tame nature for stability and prosperity. Constructed during the Great Depression and completed in 1936, this massive structure spans the **Colorado River** between Arizona and Nevada, creating **Lake Mead**, the largest reservoir in the United States.

At the time of its completion, the Hoover Dam was the tallest dam in the world and a beacon of American ambition. Standing 726 feet high and 1,244 feet long, it was built with over **3.25 million cubic yards of concrete**—enough to pave a road from San Francisco to New York City. But the dam was more than an engineering marvel; it was a symbol of hope and renewal during one of the darkest economic periods in American history.

The Hoover Dam had three primary purposes: **flood control**, **hydroelectric power generation**, and **water storage** for irrigation. The Colorado River, which once flooded unpredictably, now flowed under human command, enabling the agricultural development of vast arid regions in the American Southwest. Cities like **Las Vegas**, **Phoenix**, and **Los Angeles** grew and flourished in part because of the dam's contribution to regional stability and infrastructure.

Engineering the dam required solving unprecedented challenges. The searing desert temperatures made construction grueling, and the massive volume of concrete needed to be cooled as it set—a problem engineers solved by embedding cooling pipes through the structure and pumping ice-cold water. Innovative systems were devised to divert the river during construction, and enormous intake towers were built to channel water through hydroelectric turbines.

More than just a dam, it became an icon of American perseverance and ingenuity. The art deco design of its towers, tunnels, and generators was not merely functional but symbolic, conveying strength, modernity, and elegance.

For many, visiting the Hoover Dam was a pilgrimage to the future—a place where people saw what civilization could achieve through engineering.

Even today, it provides electricity to millions, irrigates fields, and supplies drinking water to multiple states. Amid growing concerns over water scarcity and climate change, the Hoover Dam also highlights the complexities of managing natural resources in the modern age.

Skyscrapers: Reaching for the Sky

While dams and canals show humanity's ability to reshape earth and water, **skyscrapers** symbolize our desire to **reach upward**, creating vertical cities that maximize limited space and project ambition toward the sky. The modern skyscraper is not merely a tall building—it is a triumph of architecture, engineering, and urban planning, rising from innovations in steel construction, elevator technology, and material science.

The roots of the skyscraper can be traced to **late 19th-century Chicago**, after the Great Fire of 1871 devastated much of the city. Faced with a rapidly growing population and limited land, architects and engineers began to build upward. The **Home Insurance Building**, completed in 1885, is often cited as the world's first skyscraper, standing at 10 stories tall with a steel frame that supported its weight.

This innovation made it possible to construct buildings that rose well beyond the limitations of masonry and brick. The introduction of the **elevator**, refined by **Elisha Otis**, ensured that these tall structures could be easily navigated, ushering in a new urban reality.

By the early 20th century, cities like **New York** and **Chicago** were in the midst of a skyscraper boom. Structures like the **Empire State Building**, completed in 1931, and the **Chrysler Building** became symbols of modernity, capitalism, and human aspiration. The Empire State Building, rising 1,454 feet with its antenna, held the record as the tallest building in the world for nearly 40 years.

Modern skyscrapers have pushed even further. The **Burj Khalifa** in **Dubai**, currently the world's tallest building, soars over 2,700 feet into the sky. These structures use cutting-edge technologies to counter wind forces, seismic activity, and energy demands. New materials like **carbon fiber composites**, and sustainable systems like **green roofs** and **smart glass**, are turning skyscrapers into eco-efficient urban hubs.

Skyscrapers have become more than engineering achievements—they are cultural signifiers. From the financial power of Wall Street to the innovation hubs of Asia, they represent not just shelter, but identity, prestige, and vision. Cities compete for skyline supremacy as a marker of economic and architectural distinction.

However, the rise of these vertical giants also invites reflection. As populations grow and urbanization accelerates, skyscrapers serve as laboratories for the cities of tomorrow. How we build and design these mega-structures will influence sustainability, social equity, and quality of life in a rapidly urbanizing world.

7.2 Innovations in Transport and Mobility

The story of human civilization is inseparable from the story of movement. From the earliest footpaths to modern spacecraft, the ability to move people and goods across distances has defined how societies grow, interact, and evolve. Throughout history, breakthroughs in transportation have not merely changed how we get from one place to another—they have shaped economies, redrawn political boundaries, and redefined what it means to be connected. Among the most transformative of these innovations are the **evolution of the airplane**, the development of **railway systems**, and the technological marvels behind **space exploration vehicles**.

The Airplane: From Dream to Dominion of the Skies

The concept of human flight long resided in the realm of myth and aspiration. From Icarus' wings to Leonardo da Vinci's flying machines, the desire to conquer the skies stirred the imagination for centuries. It was not until **December 17, 1903**, however, that **Orville and Wilbur Wright** made the dream a reality. Their Flyer lifted off the sands of **Kitty Hawk, North Carolina**, marking the first powered, sustained, and controlled flight in a heavier-than-air aircraft.

From this modest 12-second flight, aviation took off—literally and metaphorically. The first decades of the 20th century saw rapid experimentation, and by **World War I**, airplanes had become instruments of war and reconnaissance. Postwar periods saw the advent of **commercial aviation**, with early passenger flights gradually becoming safer, faster, and more reliable.

Technological milestones continued to redefine the field. The invention of the **jet engine** in the 1930s and 40s propelled aviation into the modern era, making possible the development of aircraft like the **Boeing 707** and the **Concorde**. The jet age shrank continents and brought intercontinental travel within reach for millions. Airports became new global gateways, and the airplane emerged as the backbone of globalization—connecting business, families, and cultures with unprecedented speed.

Beyond utility, aviation has been symbolic. Charles Lindbergh's solo transatlantic flight, Amelia Earhart's daring journeys, and the supersonic spectacle of the Concorde all capture the imagination. Airplanes also spurred the creation of a vast support infrastructure—from air traffic control systems to global logistics networks—that remains essential to the functioning of the modern world.

Today, the push toward sustainable aviation—with **electric planes**, **hydrogen propulsion**, and **supersonic renewables**—signals yet another chapter. As we move into an era of climate-conscious innovation, the history of flight reminds us of our relentless drive to overcome gravity and distance.

Railway Systems: Tracks That Built Nations

If the airplane revolutionized the skies, the **railway system** transformed the very ground beneath our feet. Railroads were the arteries of the **Industrial Revolution**, carrying coal, steel, people, and ideas across landscapes that were previously insurmountable by foot, horse, or cart. More than a means of transport, railways helped forge national identities and stimulate economic development on an unprecedented scale.

The origins of modern rail transport date back to **early 19th-century England**, where **George Stephenson**'s steam-powered locomotives changed everything. The **Liverpool and Manchester Railway**, opened in 1830, became the first fully operational passenger railway line. Its success sparked a railway boom across Europe and North America, with thousands of miles of track laid in mere decades.

In the **United States**, the **Transcontinental Railroad**, completed in 1869, linked the Atlantic and Pacific coasts, dramatically altering migration patterns, commerce, and the expansion of territories. It symbolized the taming of the American frontier and allowed for the mass movement of people and goods across vast distances, contributing to the rise of cities and the integration of national markets.

In **India**, the introduction of railways under British colonial rule in the mid-19th century became both a tool of imperial control and a foundation for economic transformation. The railway system, still one of the largest in the world today, knitted together a culturally and geographically diverse subcontinent.

Over time, technological advancements transformed rail travel. The shift from steam to **electric and diesel engines**, the introduction of **high-speed rail** in countries like Japan (with the **Shinkansen**) and France (with the **TGV**), and innovations in **magnetic levitation** (Maglev) systems have pushed the limits of speed and efficiency.

Railways remain more than historical curiosities. In today's age of urban congestion and environmental concern, rail transport offers sustainable solutions for mass mobility. Metro systems, intercity trains, and transcontinental freight lines continue to play a vital role in modern life, connecting people not just physically, but socially and economically.

Space Vehicles: Reaching for the Infinite

Of all the modes of transportation ever conceived, none have captured the imagination quite like the machines that leave Earth entirely. **Space exploration vehicles** represent the pinnacle of engineering ambition—machines designed not only to travel vast distances but to survive and function in the most hostile environment known to humanity: outer space.

The launch of **Sputnik 1** by the Soviet Union in 1957 marked the beginning of the **space age**. This simple satellite transmitted beeps back to Earth, but it sent a powerful message: humanity had entered a new frontier. This milestone triggered the **Space Race**, a Cold War contest that culminated in the **Apollo 11** mission, where **Neil Armstrong** and **Buzz Aldrin** became the first humans to walk on the Moon in 1969.

Since then, the evolution of space vehicles has followed several pathways. Unmanned probes like **Voyager**, **Cassini**, and **Perseverance** have explored distant planets, moons, and asteroids, sending back data that has reshaped our understanding of the solar system. Meanwhile, crewed spacecraft—from the **Space Shuttle** to the **International Space Station (ISS)**—have enabled long-duration human presence in orbit.

Engineering space vehicles requires pushing the limits of material science, navigation, propulsion, and safety systems. Rockets must escape Earth's gravity at over 28,000 kilometers per hour, shield passengers from cosmic radiation, and perform flawlessly in zero-gravity environments.

Now, with the emergence of **private spaceflight** companies such as **SpaceX**, **Blue Origin**, and **Virgin Galactic**, the concept of space as a public venture is shifting toward commercial frontiers. Reusable rockets, lunar colonization plans, and visions of Mars settlements bring with them both exciting potential and ethical questions.

Space vehicles are not just technological marvels—they are cultural symbols. They represent our curiosity, our willingness to risk, and our desire to understand the cosmos. As we look forward to missions beyond Earth orbit, these vehicles remind us that engineering is the bridge between imagination and discovery.

7.3 Infrastructure as Cultural Landmarks

While engineering achievements often prioritize function, some infrastructures transcend their utilitarian purpose to become icons of human identity, ingenuity, and aspiration. These **bridges**, **subway systems**, and **renewable energy projects** are more than structures—they are landmarks that encapsulate cultural values, reflect societal priorities, and shape the rhythms of daily life.

Bridges: Connecting More Than Land

Few structures are as poetically symbolic as bridges. They connect not only physical spaces but also people, cultures, and histories. A bridge, in its most elegant form, is a statement of unity over separation.

Consider the **Golden Gate Bridge** in **San Francisco**. Completed in 1937, its sweeping Art Deco design and distinctive orange-red hue have made it a global icon. Beyond aesthetics, it overcame daunting engineering challenges—such as building over the swirling currents of the Golden Gate Strait—and became a symbol of American innovation during the Great Depression.

In **Europe**, the **Millau Viaduct** in southern France is a more recent marvel. Opened in 2004, it is one of the tallest bridges in the world, soaring gracefully over the Tarn River Valley. Its minimalistic design belies immense complexity, demonstrating how engineering and architecture can coexist in harmony with natural landscapes.

Meanwhile, historic bridges like **London's Tower Bridge**, **Florence's Ponte Vecchio**, or **Istanbul's Bosphorus Bridge** tell stories of commerce, empire, and coexistence. Bridges often evolve into national emblems, appearing in artwork, currency, and collective memory. They remind us that infrastructure can be beautiful and symbolic, not just functional.

Subway Systems: The Arteries of Modern Cities

Where bridges span space, **subway systems** burrow beneath it, moving millions every day in an intricate dance of time and efficiency. Often overlooked, subway systems are the lifeblood of modern cities, enabling dense urban living and supporting economic dynamism.

The **London Underground**, opened in 1863, was the first of its kind. Since then, cities around the world have developed their own underground networks—each reflecting the unique character of its environment. The **New York City Subway**, with its gritty charm and 472 stations, pulses with the city's relentless energy. The **Paris Métro**, with its Art Nouveau entrances and punctual service, blends functionality with aesthetic flair.

In **Tokyo**, **Seoul**, and **Shanghai**, metro systems are marvels of technological efficiency, handling enormous passenger volumes with precision and automation. Stations double as shopping centers, art galleries, and even emergency shelters, reflecting the evolving role of public space.

But subways also represent deeper societal values—accessibility, equality, and sustainability. They offer alternatives to car culture and reduce urban congestion, lowering emissions and reshaping how cities breathe and grow.

Renewable Energy Projects: Building a Sustainable Future

In the 21st century, the most culturally significant infrastructure may not be visible from the surface at all—but rather found in the **wind farms**, **solar arrays**, and **hydroelectric dams** transforming our relationship with energy. These **renewable energy projects** represent a fundamental shift in how humanity powers itself, moving away from fossil fuels toward cleaner, more sustainable sources.

Projects like **China's Three Gorges Dam**, **Germany's Energiewende** (energy transition), and **Denmark's offshore wind farms** are redefining national priorities and global leadership. In deserts, vast **solar farms** capture the sun's power to light entire cities. In rural regions, **community wind turbines** empower local grids and decentralize control.

These infrastructures are more than power plants—they are **monuments to responsibility**, declarations of intent to future generations. They symbolize a cultural pivot toward long-term thinking and environmental stewardship. Just as aqueducts once defined the ingenuity of Rome, or cathedrals embodied spiritual devotion, renewable energy projects may come to represent our era's most profound values.

7.4 Ancient Construction Tools and Techniques

Egyptian Copper Chisels, Roman Cranes and Pulleys, Incan Stone and Rope Technologies

Every towering monument of antiquity began not with a divine miracle or a legendary hero, but with a set of human hands and a humble tool. From the deserts of Egypt to the hills of Rome and the mountains of the Andes, ancient builders relied on ingenuity, observation, and craft to transform raw landscape into enduring architecture. Their achievements—temples, roads, fortresses, aqueducts—still astonish us today. Yet, behind the grandeur lie stories of the tools and techniques that made these wonders possible.

In this chapter, we uncover the often-overlooked brilliance of ancient construction: how Egyptian copper chisels shaped the stones of the pyramids; how Roman engineers devised cranes and pulley systems to lift massive weights with precision; and how Incan stonemasons, with neither iron nor wheels, achieved seamless joints that still defy modern explanation. These tools and techniques weren't just mechanical—they were reflections of how each civilization saw the world and their place in it.

Egyptian Copper Chisels: Precision in the Desert

Few structures in human history are as iconic—or as mysterious—as the pyramids of Egypt. For centuries, they have stood as monumental expressions of engineering prowess, astronomical knowledge, and state power. But for all their grandeur, their construction was rooted in simple, manual tools—none more emblematic than the **copper chisel**.

In the third millennium BCE, when the Great Pyramid of Giza was rising under Pharaoh Khufu, Egypt had not yet entered the Iron Age. Instead, their tools were forged from copper, a soft metal by modern standards, but sufficient for the limestone and sandstone commonly used in construction. Harder stones, like granite, presented more of a challenge, yet even here, copper—combined with abrasive materials and relentless human labor—proved effective.

The basic process of stone dressing involved striking copper chisels against rock faces to shape blocks into the desired size and angle. Workers used stone hammers and dolerite pounders to rough out the forms, and then finer chisels to achieve smooth, flat surfaces. For particularly hard stones, sand mixed with water was used as an abrasive in combination with copper tools to wear down surfaces gradually. The attention to detail was astonishing. Blocks in the core of pyramids were roughly hewn, but those lining the interior chambers or outer casing stones were cut with such accuracy that even a knife blade couldn't pass between them.

Chisels had to be frequently resharpened, a task done at nearby workshops where blacksmiths heated and hammered the copper tools back into usable form. This cycle of dulling and sharpening reveals an underappreciated part of Egyptian construction: the **logistical ecosystem** behind the building sites. Tool production, maintenance, labor organization, and material transport formed a vast and coordinated system.

Far from being primitive, these tools represent a level of adaptability and patience that is difficult to replicate today. They embody a civilization willing to spend decades shaping stone with modest implements—driven not by haste, but by legacy.

Roman Cranes and Pulleys: Lifting the Empire

If the Egyptians taught the world how to build from the ground up, the **Romans mastered how to build upward**—faster, stronger, and more efficiently than ever before. The secret to their success was not merely architectural vision but mechanical invention. Among their most important tools were cranes and pulleys—simple machines that allowed them to raise immense weights with calculated precision.

The Roman crane, known in Latin as *polyspaston* or *trispaston*, was a marvel of practical engineering. It combined a vertical mast with a horizontal jib (or beam), ropes, and a system of pulleys operated by human or animal power. The pulley system, using the principles of mechanical advantage, allowed builders to lift stones many times heavier than what a person could manage alone. Some cranes also included **treadwheel mechanisms**—massive wooden wheels that workers walked inside, like giant hamster wheels, turning the axle and winding up the rope.

Cranes were used extensively across the Roman world—in the construction of aqueducts, temples, amphitheaters, and city walls. They allowed for rapid construction and the lifting of heavy architectural elements, such as columns, capitals, and entablatures. At sites like the Colosseum and the Baths of Caracalla, massive stone blocks weighing several tons were hoisted into place with astonishing accuracy.

The real brilliance of the Roman crane wasn't just its raw power—it was its **modularity and mobility**. Cranes could be assembled and disassembled on-site, moved to where they were needed, and adjusted in size according to the task. Roman builders understood how to scale tools to match their ambitions.

Supporting the cranes was a network of auxiliary tools: **block and tackle systems**, **winches**, **capstans**, and **sheaves**. Each device multiplied human effort, spreading loads and ensuring stability. Romans also made extensive use of **scaffolding, plumb bobs, groma for surveying**, and **measuring rods**—tools that laid the foundation for their symmetrical, grid-based city layouts and their reputation for architectural order.

Roman engineering was, above all, about optimization. They didn't just build to impress—they built to last, to expand, and to integrate new territories into the empire. The tools they developed weren't only used in Rome; they traveled with legions and laborers, reshaping the Mediterranean world and beyond.

Incan Stone and Rope Technologies: Mastery Without Metal

High in the Andes, far from the copper chisels of Egypt or the ironwork of Rome, the **Inca civilization** built with a brilliance that defies expectations. They had no written language, no draft animals for heavy labor, no wheels, and no iron or steel tools—yet they constructed one of the most advanced and enduring infrastructures in the ancient world.

At the heart of Incan construction was their exceptional **stoneworking technique**. The most famous examples, such as the walls of Cusco and Machu Picchu, feature **polygonal masonry**—stones fitted together with such precision that no mortar was needed. These joints are not simple squares or rectangles but irregular, multi-angled shapes. Each stone was shaped to interlock perfectly with its neighbors, creating walls that were both durable and **earthquake-resistant**. The method was not only functional but deeply aesthetic, reflecting the Incan appreciation for harmony with nature.

But how were these stones shaped and moved without metal tools? The Incas used hammerstones—dense river stones harder than the stones they were working on—to slowly chip away and shape the blocks. They relied on **abrasion techniques**, using sand and water to smooth surfaces. The work was slow, laborious, and often communal, relying on coordinated effort rather than speed.

For transport and lifting, the Incas employed ingenious methods based on **rope technologies**. They constructed **suspension bridges** made of woven grass rope, strong enough to support people, animals, and supplies. These bridges spanned deep gorges and were maintained regularly by local communities, a practice that continues in parts of Peru today.

To move large stones, they used **wooden rollers**, **levers**, and coordinated **human labor**. Historical accounts from Spanish chroniclers describe massive stones being dragged by hundreds of workers in unison, guided by rhythmic chants and careful coordination. Ropes and pulleys—though rudimentary—were crucial for hoisting and positioning.

Beyond tools, the Incas understood **terrain**. They built terraces into mountain slopes, stabilizing hillsides for agriculture and construction alike. Their roads, paved with stone and stretching over 24,000 miles, included drainage systems, stairways, and retaining walls. These were not only feats of civil engineering but the arteries of a vast and organized empire.

Perhaps most remarkable is the Incan emphasis on **natural integration**. Their stones seem to grow out of the landscape, their buildings hugging contours rather than imposing upon them. Their tools and techniques, while less metallic or mechanized, reflect a different kind of mastery: one of harmony, patience, and adaptation.

Timeless Techniques, Enduring Vision

The construction tools of ancient civilizations were more than technical instruments—they were **extensions of cultural values**, shaped by geography, material availability, and worldview. Egyptian copper chisels speak to a people willing to spend decades perfecting the afterlife's architecture. Roman cranes and pulleys reveal a society obsessed with order, efficiency, and permanence. Incan stonework, meticulous and mortarless, shows a civilization in tune with the land and the power of collaboration.

These tools did not just build structures—they built legacies. They enabled roads, temples, cities, and empires. They carried not only stone but **meaning**, reflecting how societies thought, organized, and dreamed. And perhaps most tellingly, many of these tools and techniques—though thousands of years old—still inform modern practices today. We still use chisels and pulleys. We still marvel at earthquake-resistant joints and community-built bridges.

In the end, it's easy to stand before a pyramid, a coliseum, or a mountain city and marvel at its scale. But the real wonder lies in the **tools**, **hands**, and **minds** that made it possible. These ancient instruments remind us that innovation doesn't always come in the form of sleek machines or digital design. Sometimes, it's a copper chisel, a wooden treadwheel, or a perfectly placed stone—simple tools, used with uncommon wisdom.

7.5 Machines of the Industrial Age

The Industrial Age arrived not with a single invention but with a storm of moving parts. Gears turned, pistons pumped, levers snapped into place—and the world was transformed. In just a few generations, humankind transitioned from handcraft to machine power, from horse-drawn carriages to locomotives, from candlelight to gaslamps, and eventually to electric cities that never slept. This was not just technological advancement; it was a wholesale reimagining of how labor, production, and communication functioned in society.

At the heart of this upheaval were the machines themselves—marvels of design that not only multiplied human effort but redefined what was possible. They didn't just speed things up; they changed how people lived, worked, and thought. In this chapter, we'll examine three foundational machines of the Industrial Age: the **steam engine**, the **textile loom**, and the **printing press** (along with its sleeker cousin, the typewriter). Each one carved deep grooves into the path of modernity, and together, they turned the wheels of a new era.

Steam Engines: Fire, Pressure, and Progress

If there was one machine that came to symbolize the Industrial Revolution, it was the **steam engine**. Fueled by coal and fire, it was not just a marvel of mechanics—it was the beating heart of industrial capitalism, drawing up coal from the mines, powering textile factories, and driving the locomotives and ships that stitched continents together.

The concept of using steam to perform mechanical work had ancient precedents. As far back as the 1st century CE, the Greek inventor Hero of Alexandria described a simple steam-powered device known as an **aeolipile**—a spinning ball driven by escaping steam. But it wasn't until the 18th century that steam became truly harnessed for practical, sustained use.

The turning point came with **Thomas Newcomen**, whose early atmospheric engine, developed around 1712, was designed to pump water out of coal mines. It was cumbersome and inefficient, but it worked—and more importantly, it laid the groundwork for future improvements.

Enter **James Watt**, the Scottish engineer who refined and revolutionized steam power. In the 1760s and 70s, Watt introduced key innovations: a separate condenser that reduced energy waste, rotary motion mechanisms, and throttle valves for better control. His partnerships with manufacturers and industrialists helped steam engines spread across Britain and beyond, powering everything from cotton mills to iron foundries.

The mechanics of a steam engine are deceptively straightforward. Water is boiled to produce steam, which expands under pressure. This steam pushes against a piston or turns a turbine, converting thermal energy into kinetic energy. The controlled release of pressure—through carefully engineered valves and chambers—turns what was once dangerous, chaotic force into reliable, repeatable power.

But the true legacy of the steam engine lies not in its technical specs, but in its **consequences**. It **decoupled production from natural forces**. Before steam, factories had to be built near fast-flowing rivers to power water wheels. With steam, industry could flourish anywhere coal could be brought. Cities exploded in size. Rural populations migrated en masse to work in smoky, soot-laced factory towns. Railways and steamships shrank the world. Supply chains lengthened, but delivery times shortened.

The steam engine didn't just move machines—it moved empires. It powered colonial expansion, enabled mass transportation, and rewrote the global economy. And though it would eventually give way to internal combustion and electricity, its blueprint lives on in turbines, generators, and any system where pressure becomes motion.

Textile Looms: Mechanizing the Fabric of Society

Before the roar of steam, the clatter of the **loom** was the soundtrack of industrialization. The textile industry was among the first to fully mechanize, and in doing so, it became both the symbol and the engine of early industrial progress. From spinning jennies to power looms, these machines transformed fibers into fortunes—and homespun economies into factory systems.

Weaving, of course, is ancient. For millennia, it was the work of hands and feet—women at home or artisans in guild workshops, manipulating warp and weft with patience and skill. But with the dawn of mechanization, this delicate art became industrial science.

The first major breakthrough came in the 18th century with the **flying shuttle**, invented by **John Kay** in 1733. This device allowed a single weaver to operate a loom at much greater speed by launching the shuttle—carrying the weft yarn—across the warp threads automatically. Productivity soared, and so did demand for thread, prompting the invention of faster spinning machines like the **Spinning Jenny** (James Hargreaves, 1764) and **Arkwright's water frame** (1769).

But the real shift came with the introduction of the **power loom** by **Edmund Cartwright** in the 1780s. Powered initially by water and later by steam, the power loom transformed weaving into a mechanized, high-volume operation. Now, what once took a skilled hand hours to produce could be replicated thousands of times a day by machines, operated by low-wage laborers—often women and children—in vast textile mills.

The internal mechanics of the power loom were complex but ingenious. Patterns of movement had to be precisely timed: lifting warp threads, passing the shuttle, beating the weft into place—all choreographed with camshafts, pulleys, and tension gears. Later innovations, such as **Jacquard's punch card system** (1804), allowed for automated pattern weaving and are considered precursors to modern computing.

The effects of this mechanization were enormous. Cloth became cheaper and more widely available. Factory work replaced cottage industry. Entire cities—like Manchester and Lowell—grew around textile production. Labor movements emerged in response to harsh conditions and exploitative practices. The social fabric was being rewoven as fast as the physical one.

The loom, then, was not merely a machine—it was a **social fulcrum**. It redefined labor, gender roles, consumer culture, and even colonial economics (British mills, for instance, relied heavily on raw cotton grown on enslaved labor in the Americas). Through the loom, the threads of industry, empire, and everyday life were tightly interwoven.

Typewriters and Printing Presses: Voices Multiply

As steam turned wheels and looms spun threads, another revolution was quietly unfolding—one of **language, communication, and literacy**. The printed word, once the domain of scribes and scholars, began to reach broader audiences thanks to mechanical presses and eventually the typewriter: a machine that gave individuals the power to write with the permanence of print.

Though **Johannes Gutenberg's** 15th-century press had already transformed Europe by enabling the mass production of books, it was in the 19th century that printing presses truly became industrial machines. With steam power and iron construction, presses could now produce thousands of pages per hour. Newspapers, once weekly or monthly, became **daily**, reporting on politics, science, war, and culture with unprecedented speed.

The **steam-powered press**, like those designed by **Friedrich Koenig** in the early 1800s, introduced rotating cylinders and automatic inking, greatly increasing efficiency. Soon after, the **Linotype machine** (1884) automated the setting of type, revolutionizing how text was assembled and published.

Parallel to this evolution was the rise of the **typewriter**, a more personal and intimate machine. The first commercially successful model, the **Sholes and Glidden typewriter**, entered the market in 1874. With its distinctive QWERTY keyboard and striking mechanism, it allowed for uniform, legible text—and democratized the act of writing. Office work changed forever. Authors, secretaries, clerks, and journalists embraced the machine, and it quickly became a staple of the modern workplace.

Typewriters also opened doors. For many women, typing offered one of the first white-collar job opportunities. The "typewriter girl" became a fixture in 19th- and early 20th-century offices—a symbol of modernity, gender shift, and the evolving labor market.

Both presses and typewriters served the same cultural function: **amplifying voices**. They enabled the spread of ideas, the rise of public discourse, and the birth of mass media. They fueled revolutions—political, intellectual, and artistic. Newspapers gave rise to public opinion; typewriters gave rise to individual authorship.

Importantly, these machines didn't only preserve language—they **shaped it**. The brevity demanded by newspaper columns, the formality encouraged by typed documents, the speed of transcription—they all influenced how people communicated, structured arguments, and told stories. Even today, echoes of the typewriter linger in our keyboards, our word processors, our inboxes.

Machines That Made Modernity

The steam engine roared, the loom clattered, the typebars clicked. Each machine was a gear in the larger engine of the Industrial Age, spinning out not just goods but entire **ways of life**. They redefined time—dividing it into shifts, deadlines, and production cycles. They redefined labor—mechanizing skill, centralizing work, and commodifying effort. And they redefined power—economic, political, and cultural.

What unites these machines is their dual nature: they were tools, but also **symbols**. They stood for progress, efficiency, and control. Yet they also provoked anxiety—about displacement, inequality, and the pace of change. The Industrial Age was not an era of simple optimism. It was complex, noisy, and full of contradiction. It built great wealth and sowed unrest. It enabled genius and demanded sacrifice.

But in these machines, we glimpse the heart of modern civilization: the drive to invent, the need to organize, the hope to connect. Whether stoking a furnace, threading a loom, or striking a key, people used machines not just to produce—but to **transform**. And the world, once changed, never looked back.

Chapter 8: Communication and Information Revolution

"The medium is the message." — Marshall McLuhan

8.1 Transformative Communication Technologies

Communication is the bedrock of human society. It enables us to share ideas, express emotions, build communities, pass down knowledge, and shape culture. For most of history, communication was bound by physical proximity—voices could only carry so far, messages had to be carried by foot, horse, or ship. But beginning in the 19th century, a series of revolutionary innovations fundamentally redefined how humans connect. These **transformative communication technologies** compressed time and space, turning vast distances into mere moments and laying the foundation for our hyper-connected world. From the **telegraph and telephone** to **radio and television**, and ultimately to the **internet**, each advancement catalyzed profound changes in culture, politics, and human interaction.

The Telegraph and Telephone: Wiring the World

The first great leap came with the **telegraph**, a system that allowed coded messages to travel instantly over wires. Invented in the early 19th century, it was **Samuel Morse's** version—coupled with his development of **Morse code**—that gained widespread adoption. In 1844, the first official telegraph message, "What hath God wrought," was sent from Washington, D.C., to Baltimore. It marked the beginning of a new era.

Before the telegraph, long-distance communication relied on messengers, signal fires, or the postal service—all subject to delay and uncertainty. The telegraph shattered these limitations. For the first time, information could move faster than a person. Governments, businesses, and news organizations were among the first to embrace it, transforming how wars were fought, markets were managed, and events were reported.

The **transatlantic cable**, completed in 1866, connected Europe and North America with undersea wires, collapsing intercontinental communication time from weeks to minutes. News from London could reach New York in real time, changing diplomacy, finance, and journalism forever. Newspapers became more immediate, stock prices could be updated across continents, and empires expanded their administrative reach.

Yet the telegraph, for all its marvel, was impersonal and limited to trained operators. The next leap—one that would bring voice to the wire—came with the **telephone**. Patented by **Alexander Graham Bell** in 1876, the telephone made it possible for individuals to speak directly across great distances. No more waiting for decoded dots and dashes—people could now hear each other in real time, complete with tone, emotion, and nuance.

The telephone began as a curiosity for the elite, but it rapidly became a staple of modern life. By the early 20th century, telephone lines were being strung across cities and rural landscapes alike. Switchboard operators—mostly women—became a common feature of the communication economy, connecting calls manually in the early years. Telephony also gave rise to powerful new businesses. Companies like **AT&T** (American Telephone and Telegraph) grew into global giants, managing the infrastructure that kept voices moving around the world.

More than a convenience, the telephone redefined social dynamics. It changed how families stayed in touch, how emergencies were reported, how businesses were managed, and even how romantic relationships evolved. It also restructured the design of homes, cities, and offices, as people came to expect near-instant access to one another.

Together, the telegraph and telephone laid the groundwork for the **electronic communication age**—an age in which ideas could travel without a body, where sound could leap across the globe at the speed of electricity.

Radio and Television: Broadcasting to the Masses

While the telegraph and telephone revolutionized one-to-one communication, the advent of **radio and television** opened the door to one-to-many communication—a single voice or image broadcast simultaneously to millions. This shift from personal to mass communication had far-reaching cultural, political, and psychological effects. For the first time, societies could be unified through shared experiences transmitted through invisible waves.

Radio emerged in the late 19th century, building on the work of scientists like **Heinrich Hertz**, **Nikola Tesla**, and **Guglielmo Marconi**. By the early 20th century, radio had become a medium for transmitting not just Morse code, but **voice and music**. Marconi's transatlantic signal in 1901 demonstrated its global potential.

In its early days, radio was used for military and maritime purposes—sending messages to ships at sea, coordinating operations in wartime. But soon it became a tool of **public entertainment and information**. In the 1920s, the rise of commercial broadcasting saw radio sets entering households across Europe and the Americas. Families would gather in living rooms to listen to music, sports, serialized dramas, and breaking news.

Perhaps no other medium has captured the intimacy and immediacy of human emotion like radio. During the **Great Depression**, **Franklin D. Roosevelt's "Fireside Chats"** reassured anxious American citizens. During **World War II**, radio broadcasts brought both battle updates and morale-boosting music. In peacetime, it became the pulse of culture—birthplace of jazz and rock and roll, platform for orators and protestors, a canvas for sound-driven imagination.

Then came **television**—an innovation that would fuse the auditory and the visual, redefining mass communication yet again. Though experiments with television dated back to the 1920s, it wasn't until after **World War II** that the medium exploded into public consciousness. The 1950s are often referred to as the **"Golden Age of Television,"** as sets became affordable, and programming diversified.

TV's impact was immediate and dramatic. It turned political figures into performers, as seen in the **Kennedy-Nixon debates** of 1960. It made celebrities out of newscasters and sitcom actors alike. Events like the **moon landing**, watched by millions simultaneously, became shared historical moments—cultural glue binding people across demographics and borders.

Television also sparked debates about representation, propaganda, and consumerism. Its power to influence opinion and shape perception made it both a trusted informant and a subject of scrutiny. As color broadcasting, cable networks, and satellite TV expanded in the later 20th century, television became an almost omnipresent force—informing, entertaining, and advertising to people around the clock.

Radio and television were more than inventions; they were **mirrors and megaphones**, capable of both reflecting and directing the values of the societies they served. They shrunk the world, amplified voices, and defined generations.

The Internet: A Global Nervous System

If the telegraph was a revolution in coded distance, and the telephone a leap in personal contact, and broadcast media a stage for collective experience, then the **Internet** has been the most disruptive and encompassing transformation of all. It is not merely a communication tool—it is a platform, an infrastructure, a medium, and a virtual universe all at once.

The internet's roots lie in **ARPANET**, a U.S. military project launched in the late 1960s to develop a decentralized communication network. Early use was confined to universities and research institutions, but with the development of protocols like **TCP/IP** and later the **World Wide Web** in 1989 by **Tim Berners-Lee**, the internet became accessible to the public.

By the late 1990s, it had become a fixture in homes and workplaces. By the 2000s, it was central to commerce, education, entertainment, and daily life. By the 2010s, with the advent of smartphones and mobile broadband, it became **ubiquitous**—a digital extension of our physical lives.

The internet represents a **paradigm shift** in how information is created, accessed, and shared. Unlike radio and television, which deliver content from central sources to passive consumers, the internet is **interactive and decentralized**. Anyone with a connection can be a publisher, a curator, a creator.

Social media platforms, search engines, online marketplaces, blogs, video streaming services—all are facets of this larger ecosystem. The digital age has seen the rise of **citizen journalism**, **open-source collaboration**, and **viral culture**. Knowledge is no longer confined to libraries; it is embedded in algorithms, hyperlinks, and forums.

The internet has enabled **real-time communication** across continents, revolutionized education through platforms like MOOCs (Massive Open Online

Courses), and transformed economies with the gig economy and e-commerce. It has reshaped activism, from local protests to global movements like #MeToo and climate strikes. It has made communities more interconnected, but also more fragmented, as echo chambers and misinformation challenge shared realities.

As of today, more than **5 billion people**—over half the world's population—are online. The internet is no longer a separate realm; it is the **central nervous system** of global society. It raises urgent questions about privacy, identity, regulation, and control. Who owns data? What is truth in a world of deepfakes? How do we protect free expression without enabling harm?

The next phase—marked by **artificial intelligence**, **quantum computing**, and the **metaverse**—will only deepen the internet's entwinement with human life. But its essence remains the same: it is a tool for connection. And connection, in all its forms, remains the defining feature of civilization.

8.2 Cultural Artifacts of Media History

The evolution of communication has left behind not only technologies but **artifacts**—media creations that transcend their time to become enduring symbols of culture. These artifacts offer a lens into the values, fears, dreams, and conflicts of each era. From **early cinema** that revolutionized storytelling, to **iconic photographs** that froze moments of global significance, and the rise of **social media platforms** that redefined human interaction, each represents a critical moment in how humanity creates, shares, and preserves its collective memory.

Early Cinema: The Motion Picture Revolution

The birth of cinema in the late 19th century introduced a new language—**visual storytelling in motion**. Where literature and theater had long served as dominant narrative forms, the moving image combined them with realism and immediacy. The earliest films were short and silent, often documenting everyday events, like the Lumière brothers' famous *Arrival of a Train at La Ciotat Station* (1895). Audiences were reportedly so astonished by the realism of the incoming train that some fled the theater.

From such humble beginnings, film evolved rapidly. By the early 20th century, directors like **Georges Méliès** used cinematic techniques—cuts, dissolves, double exposures—to create fantastical stories. His 1902 film *A Trip to the Moon* showed that cinema could be more than documentary; it could be **imagination incarnate**.

Cinema quickly became a **mass entertainment medium**, with silent films drawing huge crowds across the world. Figures like **Charlie Chaplin**, **Buster Keaton**, and **Mary Pickford** became global icons. Their films transcended language and literacy, offering universal stories through gesture and expression.

The introduction of synchronized sound in the late 1920s—heralded by *The Jazz Singer*—changed everything. Film gained a voice, and with it came new genres, from musicals to gangster flicks. By the mid-20th century, cinema had become a dominant cultural force. Hollywood, Bollywood, and European art cinema each developed distinct styles and narratives, reflecting local values while influencing each other globally.

Early cinema was more than entertainment—it became a **mirror and a mold** for society. It shaped fashion, speech, attitudes, and political ideologies. Propaganda films in wartime, socially conscious dramas during the Great Depression, and romantic epics all reflected and shaped public sentiment. Films like *Metropolis* (1927), *The Birth of a Nation* (1915), or *Battleship Potemkin* (1925) were not just artistic milestones; they were tools of influence.

As an artifact, early cinema endures in film archives and retrospectives. It reminds us of how quickly a medium can gain cultural power—and how its impact reaches far beyond the screen.

Iconic Photographs: Time Captured in a Frame

While cinema shaped narratives, photography became the **keeper of moments**. A single image could tell a story more powerfully than a thousand words. As photography evolved from an expensive novelty into a widespread practice, it began to document not only faces and places, but also history in the making.

Some photographs transcend their origin to become part of **global consciousness**. Consider **"Migrant Mother"** by **Dorothea Lange** (1936), capturing the weary resolve of a woman during the Dust Bowl. Her face, etched with hardship and resilience, became emblematic of the Great Depression. Or

"Raising the Flag on Iwo Jima" by **Joe Rosenthal** (1945), which turned a moment of wartime struggle into a symbol of unity and triumph.

Then there is **"The Napalm Girl"** (1972), showing a naked, screaming Vietnamese child fleeing an airstrike—an image that deeply impacted public opinion during the Vietnam War. And **"Tank Man"** from **Tiananmen Square** (1989), a lone protester standing before a column of tanks, frozen in an act of unimaginable courage.

These photographs were not merely records of events—they became **catalysts**. They shaped public sentiment, inspired policy debates, and mobilized social movements. They exposed truths that words could not, offering immediacy and emotional resonance. A photograph's power lies in its **duality**—it is both evidence and art.

With the rise of photojournalism, especially through magazines like *Life*, *TIME*, and *National Geographic*, images became the **universal currency of news**. Readers didn't just read about events—they saw them. In the digital era, this has only intensified. A single image, now shareable in seconds, can go viral across the globe, influencing discourse in real time.

Photography has also expanded into personal life. Family albums, Polaroids, and later digital photo libraries document not just public history but private narratives. In this way, photographs are cultural artifacts at both the **macro and micro levels**, preserving the intimate and the epic alike.

Social Media Platforms: The New Agora

If cinema and photography shaped how societies saw the world, **social media** has redefined how societies see themselves—and each other. Beginning in the early 2000s with platforms like **Friendster**, **MySpace**, and soon **Facebook**, **Twitter**, **Instagram**, and **TikTok**, social media transformed communication from a top-down to a **peer-to-peer model**.

At its core, social media is an **interactive, real-time publishing platform**. It empowers individuals to broadcast thoughts, images, and videos to global audiences instantly. Unlike traditional media, which was curated and hierarchical, social media is decentralized and participatory.

The cultural consequences are vast. **News is now broken on Twitter**, discussed in threads, and debated across comment sections. **Influencers**, once a niche group, now shape global trends in fashion, politics, wellness, and more. Social media has birthed entire subcultures, memes, slang, and movements. Hashtags like **#BlackLivesMatter, #MeToo,** and **#FridaysForFuture** have become rallying cries for activism, uniting disparate voices into collective action.

But social media is also an artifact of paradoxes. It fosters both connection and isolation, truth and misinformation, liberation and surveillance. It has become a battleground for attention, with algorithms optimizing content not for truth, but for engagement.

Still, as a cultural artifact, social media is a defining force of the 21st century. It has reshaped identity, restructured language, and reframed what it means to be part of a community. In the same way that early cinema changed storytelling, social platforms have **changed the storyteller**—from director to individual.

8.3 Tangible Media: From Typewriters to Vinyl

Before the age of the internet—before wireless signals, cloud storage, and invisible data flows—there was a time when information had a weight, a texture, and a physical form. Thoughts were etched into metal, words hammered onto paper, and voices carved into grooves. Communication was not instant or effortless. It was material. It left a trail—on pulp, wax, tape, or shellac. These were the years of **tangible media**, when ideas lived in objects, and messages traveled as matter.

In this chapter, we follow the rise of tangible media from the printed word to the recorded sound. Each innovation—whether a press, a typewriter, or a vinyl disc—was not merely a technological step forward, but a **cultural event**, reshaping how people thought, worked, and connected. And though many of these technologies have been displaced by digital alternatives, their influence lingers—not just in archives and collections, but in the very ways we imagine and interact with media today.

Printing Presses: Ink, Pressure, and Permanence

The story of tangible media begins, almost inevitably, with the **printing press**. Though printing had earlier roots in East Asia, it was in mid-15th century Europe that the press, as perfected by **Johannes Gutenberg**, became a global catalyst. His movable type system, coupled with oil-based ink and a screw press adapted from winemaking, allowed for the **mass production of books**—a seismic shift in the dissemination of knowledge.

Before Gutenberg, books were precious. A single manuscript might take months, even years, to copy by hand. They were expensive, rare, and reserved for the educated elite. Gutenberg's press changed that. His printed *42-line Bible* (c. 1455) wasn't cheap, but it was reproducible—and that made all the difference.

Over the next centuries, the printing press evolved into a powerhouse of communication. In the early modern era, it enabled the rise of pamphlets and broadsheets—vehicles for religious reform, political dissent, and scientific inquiry. The Protestant Reformation, for example, owed much of its momentum to the printed word. Martin Luther's 95 Theses spread across Europe not only because of their content but because they could be **replicated and distributed** with unprecedented speed.

By the 18th and 19th centuries, innovations like steam-powered presses, rotary cylinders, and linotype machines increased output dramatically. Newspapers became daily fixtures. Novels reached mass audiences. Governments, churches, revolutionaries, and entrepreneurs all fought for control of what got printed—and who could read it.

Yet the press was never merely a utilitarian device. It had a **presence**. You could hear it clatter. You could feel the bite of type in the paper. Books and broadsheets carried the smell of ink, the texture of the page, the evidence of their manufacture. To read was to **touch an artifact**, not just absorb a message.

And even now, in a screen-saturated world, printed materials continue to hold symbolic and emotional power. A printed book still represents authority, permanence, and intention. Tangible media, in this sense, isn't only about delivery—it's about **experience**.

Telegraphs and Typewriters: When Words Gained Speed

If the printing press made mass communication possible, the **telegraph** and **typewriter** made it faster, more direct, and more immediate. These were tools of compression—technologies that stripped language of embellishment and focused it into signals, keystrokes, and codes. They didn't just convey words—they changed the way we **wrote** and **thought**.

The **telegraph**, developed in the early 19th century and widely adopted by the 1840s, marked the birth of **instant communication at a distance**. Using Morse code—a system of dots and dashes representing letters—messages could be sent along wires via electric impulses, then decoded at the receiving end. Suddenly, news could travel hundreds of miles in minutes, not days.

This was nothing short of revolutionary. Wars, elections, stock prices, weather reports—all became time-sensitive. The telegraph network rewired society. It reshaped journalism (the birth of the "inverted pyramid" style, where key facts were placed first), enabled synchronized train schedules, and laid the groundwork for global communication systems.

Yet for all its speed, the telegraph demanded **discipline**. Every word had to be considered, abbreviated, and encoded. Economy of language became paramount. In some ways, it foreshadowed the terse efficiency of emails and text messages, long before the digital age.

The **typewriter**, meanwhile, brought this mechanical precision into everyday life. First commercialized in the 1870s, with the Sholes & Glidden model, the typewriter quickly transformed how people composed documents. No longer reliant on pen and ink, writers could now **produce legible, uniform text** at high speed. Offices were restructured around typing pools. Authors and journalists gained a new tool for drafting and editing. Bureaucracies multiplied.

Typing also introduced a new rhythm and sound to the written word—the **clack of keys**, the **ding of the carriage return**, the physical effort behind each page. The layout of the keyboard, with its now-familiar QWERTY design, became second nature to millions. And with each stroke, a physical record was created—indelible, linear, and real.

The typewriter had a democratic effect. It gave individuals—especially women—new opportunities in the workplace. It helped standardize language, enforce clarity, and increase productivity. But it also shaped prose itself. Typed text tends to be **structured, concise, and visual**—a style that still influences writing today, from office memos to social media posts.

Together, the telegraph and typewriter compressed time and space. They made the world faster and more legible, and in doing so, they laid the groundwork for the **information age** that would follow.

Phonographs, Cassettes, and Vinyl Records: Capturing Sound in Substance

While print and type made language visible, the next leap in tangible media involved a **different sense entirely**: hearing. For the first time in human history, people could **record and replay sound**—preserving not only words but voices, music, emotion, and silence.

The **phonograph**, invented by **Thomas Edison** in 1877, was the first device capable of both recording and playing back sound. Using a stylus to inscribe vibrations onto a rotating cylinder wrapped in tinfoil (and later wax), it captured moments that could then be physically replayed. It was, in effect, the first machine to give **memory to machines**.

Later improvements, especially **Emile Berliner's gramophone**, introduced flat discs—what we now call **records**—which were easier to produce, store, and ship. These discs, made of shellac and eventually vinyl, became the dominant format for sound for much of the 20th century.

The mechanics were tactile and magical. A needle ran along grooves, translating tiny undulations into vibrations, which a diaphragm then turned into audible sound. No electricity was required for early models. You could wind them up, place the needle, and **listen to the past**.

What records offered was more than music—they offered **presence**. People could now hear the voice of a distant opera singer, the cry of a jazz trumpet, or the laughter of a child recorded years before. Vinyl captured not just sound but ambiance: the scratch of the needle, the warmth of analog tone, the hiss and pop of time passing.

The **cassette tape**, introduced in the 1960s by Philips, brought further portability and accessibility. For the first time, ordinary people could **record their own media**. Mixtapes became love letters. Bootlegs and demos circulated among subcultures. Dictaphones and portable recorders gave journalists and artists new freedom. And with the advent of the Walkman, music became **personal and mobile**, a soundtrack to everyday life.

Both vinyl and cassette shared one essential trait: **physical engagement**. You had to place the needle, flip the record, rewind the tape, clean the heads. Sound was not ephemeral—it was **embodied**. Albums were purchased, handled, displayed. The packaging mattered: cover art, liner notes, lyric sheets. The medium invited not just listening, but **collecting** and **curating**.

Even in the digital age, vinyl has refused to vanish. Its revival speaks to a longing for tactility, ritual, and warmth—qualities often lost in digital compression and cloud-streamed convenience. Tangible sound, it seems, still holds power.

When Media Had Weight

In tracing the arc from printing presses to vinyl records, we follow a journey not just of machines but of **media as material**. These were not invisible technologies. They **occupied space**, required effort, and engaged the senses. They connected people across time and geography, not through wires and fiber optics, but through **inked letters, punched keys**, and **grooved discs**.

Each format brought with it its own **discipline and culture**. Printing demanded typesetting and proofreading. Telegraphy required brevity and code. Typing introduced new conventions of formatting and formality. Vinyl listening encouraged patience and immersion. These weren't just methods of transmission—they were **modes of thinking**, each with its own rhythms and aesthetics.

And while many of these formats have been eclipsed by digital successors, their legacies endure. Every digital keyboard owes a debt to the typewriter. Every podcast descends from the phonograph. Every hyperlinked blog traces its ancestry to the printed page.

In a world of endless scroll and instant playback, tangible media remind us that information can be **physical, intimate**, and **slow**—and that sometimes, the weight of an object can carry more than just its content. It can carry **memory, craft**, and **connection**.

The click of a typewriter, the smell of fresh ink, the spinning of a record on a turntable—these are more than relics. They are reminders of when media had **mass**, when it mattered **where** and **how** an idea was stored. They remind us that communication was once a craft of materials, not just of messages—and in doing so, they still speak to us, loud and clear.

Chapter 9: Cultural Expressions Through Fashion

"Fashion is the armor to survive the reality of everyday life." — Bill Cunningham

9.1 Fashion as Historical Mirror

Fashion is far more than fabric stitched together for modesty or function. It is an ever-evolving canvas for human identity, status, expression, and cultural reflection. Throughout the ages, what people wore—and how they wore it—revealed the deeper undercurrents of their times: social hierarchies, economic systems, political shifts, artistic movements, and philosophical beliefs. Fashion does not exist in isolation. It responds to its surroundings and reflects the ethos of an era, making it one of the most immediate and visceral forms of cultural communication.

In this section, we explore how fashion has mirrored history through three seminal periods: the **adorned elegance of ancient Egyptian jewelry**, the **structured sophistication of Renaissance attire**, and the **radical transformations of 20th-century fashion**. Each reflects not only aesthetic preferences but also the values, structures, and aspirations of the societies that birthed them.

Egyptian Jewelry: Divine Ornamentation and Social Identity

Few civilizations have fused fashion and spirituality as seamlessly as ancient Egypt. Far from being merely decorative, Egyptian jewelry served as a **multifaceted symbol of power, belief, and social status**. To the ancient Egyptians, what adorned the body was a direct extension of identity, the divine order, and cosmic balance.

Gold, for example, was considered the flesh of the gods—especially that of the sun god **Ra**—and thus was highly prized for both religious and regal adornment.

Unlike modern societies where gold may symbolize wealth above all else, in ancient Egypt it represented **eternal life and divine power**. Royalty and high-ranking officials wore gold not just for opulence, but as a talismanic material, believed to carry protective and spiritual properties.

Jewelry in Egypt was rich with symbolism. The **scarab beetle**, a recurring motif, represented rebirth and regeneration. The **ankh** symbolized life, while **eyes of Horus** were worn for protection against evil and misfortune. These motifs were carved into amulets, rings, pectorals, and necklaces, blending beauty with metaphysical purpose.

The materials used—turquoise, lapis lazuli, carnelian—were chosen not only for their colors but for their believed spiritual attributes. **Lapis lazuli**, imported from Afghanistan, was associated with the heavens and worn to attract divine favor. Even commoners, if they could afford it, wore imitation jewelry using faience (glazed ceramic) or glass beads to emulate the wealthy, underscoring fashion's role as an aspirational tool.

Importantly, jewelry was not limited to women. **Men, including Pharaohs and priests, also adorned themselves** with elaborate collars, armlets, and headdresses. In fact, one's jewelry often communicated rank and occupation more clearly than clothing itself, which was typically made of plain linen due to Egypt's hot climate.

In life and in death, jewelry held immense importance. Elaborate adornments have been found in tombs—perhaps most famously in **Tutankhamun's burial site**, where over 5,000 precious items, including a solid gold funerary mask, were discovered. These items were not mere burial gifts; they were believed to be essential for navigating the afterlife.

In sum, ancient Egyptian fashion—rooted in divine symbolism, material reverence, and social clarity—offers a vivid portrait of a civilization that saw personal adornment as a sacred and cultural necessity.

Renaissance Attire: Power, Patronage, and the Rebirth of Aesthetics

If Egyptian adornment reflected divine symbolism, Renaissance fashion reflected **intellectual revival, artistic sophistication, and the assertion of**

earthly power. Emerging in Europe during the 14th century and flourishing in the 15th and 16th centuries, the Renaissance was a period of extraordinary cultural, political, and scientific awakening. Its fashion mirrored this explosion of ideas, capturing the complex interplay between individuality, social hierarchy, and regional identity.

The Renaissance was an age obsessed with **order, symmetry, and proportion**—values that spilled over from art and architecture into fashion. Clothing was designed to emphasize the idealized human form. Women's garments featured tight bodices and voluminous skirts, while men's tunics, padded shoulders, and codpieces projected masculinity and stature. The silhouette was meticulously engineered to reflect **beauty as geometry**, a concept rooted in classical antiquity and revived by Renaissance thinkers.

Fabrics were lush and expensive: **velvet, silk, brocade, and damask**, often imported from Asia and the Ottoman Empire. Intricate embroidery, gold thread, and hand-sewn pearls decorated garments, transforming clothing into both wearable art and financial asset. In fact, some aristocrats would bequeath garments in wills, as they held tangible value.

Fashion was a marker of **social stratification**. Sumptuary laws, enacted across Renaissance Europe, regulated who could wear what. In England, for instance, only nobles were permitted to wear specific types of fur or imported dyes like Tyrian purple. These laws not only reinforced class divisions but also protected the economic interests of domestic textile industries.

Perhaps nowhere was fashion more politicized than in the Italian city-states like **Florence**, **Venice**, and **Milan**. Families like the **Medici** understood that dressing well was as much a political statement as it was a personal choice. Clothing was used to project control, wealth, and refinement. Portraits from this era—think of **Titian's noblemen** or **Bronzino's Medici children**—often emphasize attire as a statement of dynastic legitimacy.

Women's fashion also began to reflect evolving ideas about femininity. While still confined by patriarchal norms, women gained visibility in courtly life and patronage networks. They expressed their status and sophistication through complex layered garments, elaborate hairdos, and veils. The emergence of **fashion manuals and tailors' guilds** during this period signaled the beginning of the fashion industry as a formalized institution.

Renaissance fashion was not just about aesthetics; it was **deeply enmeshed with emerging capitalism, expanding global trade, and shifting intellectual paradigms**. It was, quite literally, a cultural rebirth worn on the body.

20th Century Fashion: Revolutions in Fabric and Freedom

Few centuries have witnessed as many transformations in clothing and identity as the 20th century. Fashion during this period became a **battleground of ideologies, a stage for rebellion, and a platform for personal and collective expression**. It moved faster, reached farther, and reflected deeper shifts in society than perhaps any other time in history.

At the dawn of the century, fashion was still governed by **Edwardian and Victorian sensibilities**. Corsets, bustles, and top hats symbolized both elegance and constraint. But these began to crumble during and after **World War I**, when societal roles, especially for women, began to change dramatically. With men at war and women entering the workforce, clothing became more practical. Skirts shortened, silhouettes relaxed, and undergarments evolved.

By the 1920s, **flapper culture** emerged. Women cut their hair into bobs, wore makeup openly, and donned drop-waist dresses adorned with beads and fringe. These changes were more than stylistic—they were **acts of liberation**. The flapper represented a break from the past, embodying a new kind of femininity rooted in freedom and modernity.

The following decades each brought unique shifts. **The 1930s** reintroduced glamour during the Great Depression through Hollywood-inspired gowns. **The 1940s**, shaped by World War II, saw a return to utility: padded shoulders, knee-length skirts, and victory rolls became symbols of resilience. Rationing affected fashion, with government campaigns encouraging women to "Make Do and Mend."

The **1950s** restored postwar femininity with **Christian Dior's "New Look"**—cinched waists, full skirts, and elegance as escapism. Simultaneously, **youth culture** began to assert its influence. The rise of **blue jeans**, **leather jackets**, and **t-shirts**—once undergarments—signaled a rejection of formality and the embrace of rebellion, epitomized by icons like **James Dean** and **Marlon Brando**.

By the **1960s and 70s**, fashion became deeply political. **Miniskirts, psychedelic prints, Afro hairstyles**, and **bell bottoms** reflected a generational challenge to authority. The civil rights movement, feminist wave, and anti-war protests were all accompanied by fashion statements. Clothes were no longer just garments—they were **flags of ideology**.

In the **1980s**, power dressing emerged. Shoulder pads, bold colors, and business suits for women represented a push into male-dominated workspaces. In parallel, subcultures exploded: punk, goth, hip-hop, and preppy all developed distinct visual languages. **Madonna, Prince**, and **Run-D.M.C.** were as much style icons as musicians.

The **1990s and early 2000s** embraced minimalism, grunge, and the rise of **fast fashion**. Brands like Zara and H&M revolutionized how quickly trends could reach consumers, while fashion weeks, supermodels, and celebrity designers turned clothing into a global spectacle.

Technology and media profoundly influenced 20th-century fashion. The advent of **photography, magazines, television**, and eventually the **internet** meant that style was no longer localized—it became **globalized**, circulating with unprecedented speed and reach.

Throughout it all, 20th-century fashion reflected profound shifts: the erosion of rigid gender norms, the rise of consumerism, the democratization of style, and the empowerment of self-expression. It was a century where fashion became a voice—loud, diverse, and ever-changing.

9.2 Fashion Innovators and Icons

Fashion's evolution is punctuated by visionaries who have redefined aesthetics, challenged norms, and introduced groundbreaking concepts. Among these luminaries, **Coco Chanel** and **Yves Saint Laurent** stand out for their enduring impact. Additionally, the rise of **streetwear** has revolutionized fashion, blurring the lines between luxury and everyday attire.

Coco Chanel: Redefining Elegance

Born Gabrielle Bonheur Chanel in 1883, Coco Chanel emerged from humble beginnings to become a titan of fashion. She revolutionized women's fashion by introducing designs that prioritized comfort without sacrificing elegance. Chanel's creations, such as the iconic little black dress and the Chanel suit, broke away from the restrictive garments of the early 20th century, offering women a sense of liberation and modernity.

Beyond clothing, Chanel's influence extended to accessories and fragrances. Her introduction of costume jewelry challenged the notion that luxury was solely defined by precious gems, making fashion more accessible. The launch of Chanel No. 5 in 1921 set a new standard in perfumery, blending complex scents to create a timeless fragrance.

Chanel's legacy is not just in her designs but in her embodiment of independence and innovation. She transformed fashion into a reflection of personal identity, empowering women to express themselves beyond societal constraints.

Yves Saint Laurent: The Fusion of Art and Fashion

Yves Saint Laurent, born in 1936 in Oran, Algeria, displayed a passion for fashion from a young age. After moving to Paris, he quickly rose through the ranks, eventually becoming the head designer at the House of Dior at just 21. In 1962, he established his own fashion house, where he introduced revolutionary designs that blended art and fashion.

Saint Laurent's creations, such as the Mondrian dress, showcased his ability to draw inspiration from contemporary art. He also challenged gender norms by introducing the tuxedo suit for women, known as "Le Smoking," which became a symbol of empowerment and sophistication.

His designs often reflected cultural and societal shifts, incorporating elements from various traditions and movements. Saint Laurent's work not only redefined fashion aesthetics but also emphasized the importance of cultural dialogue within design.

Streetwear: From Subculture to Global Phenomenon

Originating in the late 20th century, streetwear emerged from the intersections of skateboarding, hip-hop, and punk cultures. Brands like Stüssy and Supreme began by catering to niche communities but eventually gained mainstream popularity, influencing global fashion trends .

Streetwear's appeal lies in its authenticity and adaptability. It challenges traditional fashion hierarchies by emphasizing individuality and community-driven aesthetics. Collaborations between streetwear brands and luxury fashion houses have further blurred the lines between high fashion and street culture, leading to a democratization of style .

Today, streetwear continues to evolve, reflecting societal changes and technological advancements, and remains a testament to fashion's dynamic nature.

9.3 Artifacts of Fashion's Future

As we look ahead, fashion is increasingly intertwined with sustainability, technology, and globalization. These elements are not only shaping design and production but also redefining consumer relationships with clothing.

Sustainable Fashion: Towards a Circular Economy

The fashion industry's environmental impact has prompted a shift towards sustainability. Brands are adopting circular models, emphasizing recycling, upcycling, and ethical sourcing. Innovations like Refiberd's AI-driven textile recycling exemplify efforts to minimize waste and promote resource efficiency.

Consumer demand for transparency and ethical practices is driving brands to reevaluate their operations. Events like Copenhagen Fashion Week have set sustainability standards, requiring participating brands to meet specific environmental criteria .

This movement towards sustainability signifies a broader cultural shift, where fashion is not only about aesthetics but also about responsibility and impact.

Wearable Technology: Integrating Fashion and Function

Advancements in technology are transforming garments into interactive experiences. Wearable tech, such as smart fabrics and accessories, offers functionalities ranging from health monitoring to augmented reality.

Designers are exploring the fusion of fashion and technology to create garments that respond to environmental stimuli or user inputs. This integration enhances user engagement and opens new avenues for personalization and innovation in fashion.

As technology becomes more embedded in daily life, wearable tech represents the convergence of utility and style, redefining the possibilities of what clothing can achieve.

Globalized Fashion: A Tapestry of Cultures

Globalization has expanded fashion's reach, allowing for a rich exchange of cultural influences. Designers draw inspiration from diverse traditions, creating collections that celebrate multiculturalism. Social media platforms have further accelerated this exchange, enabling trends to transcend borders rapidly.

However, globalization also presents challenges, such as cultural appropriation and homogenization. The industry is increasingly aware of the need for cultural sensitivity and authenticity, striving to honor the origins of the inspirations it embraces.

In this interconnected world, fashion serves as a medium for cross-cultural dialogue, fostering understanding and appreciation across communities.

Chapter 10: Symbols and Memory

"Symbols are the imaginative signposts of life." — Thomas More

10.1 Icons of Identity

In a world of language, data, and noise, symbols possess a rare and enduring clarity. They are not just visual designs or ornamental markings—they are **containers of meaning**, distilled forms of collective memory, belief, and identity. A single image can evoke centuries of history, stir emotion, and unite disparate individuals under a common cause. Among the most potent of these cultural markers are **national flags**, **coats of arms**, and the **Olympic rings**. These icons do not merely represent people or institutions—they embody the aspirations, struggles, and values of entire civilizations.

National Flags: Fabric of Nations

Few symbols are as universally recognizable or as politically charged as the **national flag**. It is a piece of cloth, but it is never just a piece of cloth. Flags are **visual proclamations of sovereignty**, sewn from historical experience and stitched with cultural narratives. Whether hoisted above embassies, draped over coffins, or waved in celebration, a flag signals more than presence—it affirms identity.

Origins and Evolution

The use of flags dates back thousands of years, with ancient civilizations such as the **Chinese, Egyptians, and Persians** employing standards or banners to signify imperial authority or military units. However, the **modern concept of a national flag**—as a symbol representing the identity of an entire people or state—took shape in the wake of the **Age of Exploration** and the **emergence of nation-states** in the 17th and 18th centuries.

The **Union Jack**, for example, combines the crosses of three patron saints— George (England), Andrew (Scotland), and Patrick (Ireland)—symbolizing the political union of their respective nations. The **Tricolore of France**, born during the French Revolution, uses three vertical bands of blue, white, and red to symbolize liberty, equality, and fraternity—values at the heart of modern democracy.

In many cases, national flags emerged from **anti-colonial movements**, reflecting the birth of new nations. The **Pan-African colors**—red, green, yellow, and black—became prominent across the continent as countries gained independence in the mid-20th century. These flags didn't just signal sovereignty; they reclaimed history and heritage from centuries of external domination.

Design and Meaning

Though often simple in appearance, flags are **deeply coded visual texts**. Every stripe, star, or color often carries meaning. In the **United States**, the thirteen stripes represent the original colonies, while the stars symbolize the current fifty states—an ever-evolving testament to federal union. In **Japan**, the white field and red sun disk reflect Shinto symbolism and the country's geographic identity as the "Land of the Rising Sun."

Some flags echo natural geography or mythology. The **Nepalese flag**, unique in its non-rectangular shape, incorporates Hindu symbols and celestial bodies to signify the Himalayas and the country's permanence. **Canada's maple leaf** is a nod to the land's natural beauty and unity amidst linguistic and cultural diversity.

These designs serve multiple functions. Flags can be **rallies for patriotism**, **tools of diplomacy**, or **signs of protest**. Their meaning can shift depending on context. For some, a flag evokes pride; for others, it might signify oppression. Their power lies precisely in their ability to condense complexity into a simple visual.

Symbolism in Action

Flags are especially prominent in moments of **national trauma or triumph**. After the September 11 attacks in 2001, the American flag became a ubiquitous symbol of resilience. When South Africa ended apartheid in 1994, it adopted a new flag that symbolized reconciliation and the forging of a united future.

During the **Olympics**, flags march before athletes, asserting national identity in a shared global space. In **protests**, flags can be burned or hoisted upside down as acts of dissent. On **Independence Days**, they become omnipresent, transforming cities into mosaics of unity.

In sum, the national flag is not static. It **lives in motion**, fluttering between pride and politics, history and hope. It is both artifact and agent—a textile embodiment of identity that continues to evolve alongside the nations it represents.

Coats of Arms: Heraldry and Legacy

While flags project identity outward in bold simplicity, **coats of arms** delve inward, telling **multilayered stories** of lineage, allegiance, and belief. These emblems, rooted in the medieval traditions of Europe, served as markers on battlefields and shields, distinguishing knights and noble houses. Over time, they evolved into sophisticated **symbols of institutional continuity**, used by governments, universities, and families.

Heraldry: The Art of Symbolic Language

The system known as **heraldry** arose in the 12th century and quickly became a visual language in its own right. Every element—a lion, a tower, a fleur-de-lis—carried specific symbolic weight. Heraldic colors, or "tinctures," also followed strict codes: **gold (or)** for generosity, **red (gules)** for warrior spirit, **blue (azure)** for loyalty.

The layout of a coat of arms was methodically structured. **The shield** bore the primary symbols. **The crest**, atop the helmet, added further distinction. **Supporters**, often animals or figures, flanked the shield, while a **motto** offered a guiding principle—such as "Dieu et mon droit" ("God and my right") used by the British monarchy.

These designs were not arbitrary. They reflected **personal narratives, political affiliations**, and **moral aspirations**. A crowned lion might symbolize royal authority; crossed swords could signal a family's martial past.

Civic and National Coats of Arms

While originally personal, coats of arms later became **symbols of collective identity**. Cities, regions, and entire nations adopted heraldic symbols as expressions of unity and governance.

The **Royal Coat of Arms of the United Kingdom**, for example, features a lion and a unicorn, representing England and Scotland respectively. The shield incorporates symbols of all four constituent nations, while the Latin motto affirms divine legitimacy and royal sovereignty.

In contrast, the **Mexican coat of arms**, displayed at the center of its flag, features an eagle perched on a cactus devouring a serpent—a mythic vision from Aztec legend representing the founding of Tenochtitlán. This powerful image binds ancient heritage to modern identity.

Even universities and religious institutions use heraldic imagery. **Harvard's seal** bears the Latin word "Veritas" (truth) across open books, signaling its mission of enlightenment. Such emblems cultivate **tradition and authority**, evoking centuries of accumulated knowledge and values.

Enduring Relevance

Though often associated with old-world aristocracy, coats of arms remain culturally potent. They appear in passports, government documents, and judicial seals. For many families, researching or reviving ancestral coats of arms is a way of reconnecting with history.

These symbols endure because they offer **continuity** in a rapidly changing world. They are visual heirlooms—rich with detail, history, and pride—reminding us of who we are and where we come from.

Olympic Rings: Global Unity in Color

Few modern symbols are as widely recognized—or as rich in idealism—as the **Olympic rings**. Designed by **Baron Pierre de Coubertin** in 1913, the five interlocking rings represent the five inhabited continents: **Africa, the Americas, Asia, Europe, and Oceania**. The six colors—blue, yellow, black, green, red, and white—were chosen because every national flag in existence at the time contained at least one of them.

What makes the Olympic rings extraordinary is not their artistic complexity but their **philosophical depth**. They symbolize **unity in diversity**, the coming together of nations not for conquest or commerce, but for shared pursuit of excellence and human potential.

Origins and Evolution

Inspired by ancient Greek traditions and Enlightenment ideals, Coubertin envisioned the modern Olympics as a space to foster **peaceful competition and mutual respect**. The rings first appeared on a flag in 1920, during the **Antwerp Games**, and have been present ever since, even through tumultuous times.

In the 20th century, the Olympics became a stage for both **international cooperation and political tension**. The rings persisted as a neutral symbol, even when games were marred by boycotts, protests, or global crises. Their presence reminded participants and spectators alike of a higher ideal.

Cultural and Political Significance

The power of the rings lies in their ability to be **both apolitical and deeply symbolic**. They are often displayed alongside national flags, creating a juxtaposition between individual and collective identity. During the **opening ceremonies**, athletes march under their nation's flag but compete under the Olympic banner—a delicate balance between pride and unity.

The Olympic rings have also served as tools for **diplomacy and visibility**. The **Paralympic movement**, the inclusion of **refugee teams**, and the increasing visibility of marginalized athletes all reflect the rings' evolving inclusiveness.

Moreover, the rings have become a commercial and cultural brand—licensed on everything from merchandise to medals—but their symbolic integrity remains largely intact. They are **not owned by any one nation** and evoke a rare sense of shared human aspiration.

10.2 Memorializing Human Experiences

Holocaust Memorials

The Holocaust, a systematic genocide perpetrated by Nazi Germany, resulted in the deaths of six million Jews and millions of other victims. Memorials dedicated to this atrocity serve not only as places of remembrance but also as stark reminders of the depths of human cruelty and the importance of vigilance against hatred.

One of the most prominent Holocaust memorials is the **Memorial to the Murdered Jews of Europe** in Berlin. Designed by architect Peter Eisenman, the memorial consists of 2,711 concrete slabs of varying heights, arranged in a grid pattern over a sloping field. The abstract design invites personal interpretation, evoking feelings of disorientation and loss, mirroring the experiences of Holocaust victims. Beneath the field lies an information center that provides historical context and personal stories, grounding the abstract experience in factual history.

In the United States, the **United States Holocaust Memorial Museum** in Washington, D.C., serves as both a memorial and an educational institution. Its architecture incorporates industrial materials and stark design elements to reflect the mechanized nature of the genocide. Exhibits include personal artifacts, photographs, and survivor testimonies, providing a comprehensive narrative of the Holocaust's horrors.

These memorials, among others worldwide, play a crucial role in preserving the memory of the Holocaust. They serve as educational tools, cautionary tales, and places for reflection, ensuring that the lessons of the past inform the present and future.

Vietnam War Memorial

The **Vietnam Veterans Memorial** in Washington, D.C., designed by Maya Lin, is a poignant tribute to the American service members who fought and died in the Vietnam War. The memorial features two black granite walls, each stretching 246 feet and inscribed with the names of over 58,000 fallen soldiers. The walls are set below ground level, creating a contemplative space that invites visitors to engage intimately with the names etched into the stone.

The design's simplicity and lack of overt symbolism were initially controversial but have since been lauded for their emotional impact. The reflective surface of the granite allows visitors to see themselves alongside the names, fostering a personal connection and a sense of shared mourning. The chronological arrangement of the names provides a historical narrative of the war's progression and the human cost involved.

This memorial has become a site of pilgrimage for veterans, families, and citizens, offering a space for healing and remembrance. It stands as a testament to the power of minimalist design in conveying profound emotional and historical weight.

Hiroshima Peace Memorial

The **Hiroshima Peace Memorial**, also known as the Atomic Bomb Dome, stands as a stark reminder of the devastation wrought by nuclear warfare. Located in Hiroshima, Japan, the structure was one of the few buildings left standing near the bomb's hypocenter after the atomic bombing on August 6, 1945. Preserved in its ruined state, the dome has become a symbol of peace and a call for the abolition of nuclear weapons.

Surrounding the dome is the **Hiroshima Peace Memorial Park**, which includes several monuments dedicated to the victims and the pursuit of peace. The **Children's Peace Monument**, inspired by the story of Sadako Sasaki, a young girl who died from radiation-induced leukemia, features a statue of a girl holding a folded paper crane, symbolizing hope and healing. The park also houses the **Peace Flame**, which has burned continuously since 1964 and will remain lit until all nuclear weapons are abolished.

These memorials serve not only as tributes to the victims but also as enduring symbols advocating for peace and the prevention of future nuclear catastrophes.

10.3 Symbols Shaping the Collective Imagination

Rosetta Stone

The **Rosetta Stone** is a granodiorite stele inscribed with a decree issued in 196 BCE during the reign of King Ptolemy V. The decree appears in three scripts: Greek, Demotic, and Egyptian hieroglyphs. Discovered in 1799 near the town of Rosetta (Rashid) in Egypt, the stone became the key to deciphering Egyptian hieroglyphs, a script that had been indecipherable for centuries.

The breakthrough came in 1822 when French scholar Jean-François Champollion announced his decipherment of the hieroglyphs, using the Greek inscription as a comparative tool. This achievement unlocked vast amounts of knowledge about ancient Egyptian language, culture, and history, laying the foundation for modern Egyptology.

Today, the Rosetta Stone resides in the British Museum, where it remains one of the most visited and studied artifacts. Its significance extends beyond its linguistic value; it symbolizes the human quest for knowledge and the importance of cross-cultural understanding in unraveling the mysteries of the past.

Statue of Liberty

The **Statue of Liberty**, officially titled "Liberty Enlightening the World," is an iconic symbol of freedom and democracy. Gifted by France to the United States in 1886, the statue was designed by sculptor Frédéric Auguste Bartholdi and built by Gustave Eiffel. Standing on Liberty Island in New York Harbor, the statue depicts a robed female figure representing Libertas, the Roman goddess of liberty.

10.4 Time Capsules and Commemorative Objects

Humanity has always had a complicated relationship with time. We are creatures both of the moment and of memory—living in the now, yet deeply concerned with what came before and what will come after. Across cultures and centuries, people have sought ways to preserve fragments of their world for future eyes: not just records of fact, but expressions of identity, values, and aspiration. These are not always in the form of grand monuments or books—they are often smaller, symbolic objects designed to carry meaning across generations.

This chapter explores the powerful human impulse to **commemorate**, **preserve**, and **speak to the future**. From the ancient burial jars of early civilizations to modern time capsules sealed beneath monuments, from coins struck to mark historical milestones to the Olympic torch passed hand to hand across nations, we look at objects that act as **bridges between eras**. Though made of metal, clay, or paper, their true material is **intention**—they are vessels for memory, designed to endure.

Ancient Burial Jars: Messages to the Afterlife

Long before the concept of a time capsule existed in modern terms, ancient peoples were already **preserving tokens of life for a different kind of audience**—not for future historians, but for the dead and the divine. Burial jars, urns, and sealed vessels found in graves across the ancient world offer some of the earliest examples of material culture created with a **long gaze**—a belief in some form of continuity after death.

In **ancient Egypt**, for example, burial practices were deeply tied to notions of eternity. Alongside mummified remains, archaeologists have uncovered **canopic jars**—elaborate vessels used to store the internal organs of the deceased. Each jar represented a protective deity and bore inscriptions meant to guide the soul in the afterlife. But more than their religious function, these jars served as **deliberate containers of human identity**—reminders of a life lived, a body once warm.

Elsewhere, in **Neolithic Europe**, large burial urns were used to store cremated remains along with fragments of tools, jewelry, or food—items believed to be needed in the next world. In **ancient China**, burial jars sometimes contained miniature replicas of homes, furniture, and servants. These weren't toys—they were imagined comforts for the spirit's journey beyond.

Across the **ancient Near East, pithoi**—large storage jars—have been unearthed in burial sites, often sealed tightly, sometimes bearing markings or symbols that suggest ritual significance. Some may have held offerings, others messages in the form of small personal artifacts: a bead, a figurine, a carving.

What all these burial containers share is an understanding of **time as layered**—not just linear. They speak to a belief in continuity between the living and the dead, in which the material world can convey emotions, obligations, and identity long after physical presence fades. Though they were never intended to be opened by us, they speak nonetheless, quietly and profoundly, across the millennia.

Time Capsules and Sealed Archives: Futures Imagined

If burial jars are directed toward the spiritual or mythic afterlife, the **modern time capsule** is an act of communication grounded in a secular kind of faith: the belief that the future will care enough to look back. Time capsules are intentional, curated collections of objects and documents meant to be opened at a specific future date—messages from one era to another, sealed in the hope that someone will be listening.

The modern idea took shape in the 20th century, though earlier precedents exist. One of the most famous early examples is the **Crypt of Civilization**, sealed at Oglethorpe University in Georgia in 1940. It contains microfilm archives, household items, scientific instruments, and recordings of contemporary voices—all intended for the year **8113 CE**. Its creators aimed to preserve a snapshot of mid-20th-century American life in a time-proof chamber of inert gas and stainless steel.

Since then, time capsules have appeared under cornerstone ceremonies, inside walls of public buildings, and buried beneath monuments. Many are planned to be opened within a century; others extend thousands of years. Their contents range from the mundane (newspapers, coins, photos) to the aspirational (essays, predictions, cultural artifacts). Some capsules are created by governments or institutions; others are grassroots or even playful—classroom projects, personal collections, community initiatives.

Beyond the physical object, the time capsule reflects a profound emotional and philosophical gesture. It assumes continuity, not collapse. It imagines that **our world is worth remembering**, that our choices, technologies, and everyday lives contain some lasting relevance. It often reflects both **pride and anxiety**—a desire to show our best face to the future, even as we worry whether that future will arrive at all.

Closely related to the time capsule are **sealed archives**—officially restricted collections that are preserved but inaccessible for decades or even centuries. The Vatican Apostolic Archive, for example, holds centuries of papal correspondence and records, much of it still off-limits. In France, certain state documents remain sealed for 100 years. These archives are time capsules with a legal lock, guarding not only objects but political secrets, cultural shifts, and the evolving story of governance.

Whether created by schoolchildren or states, time capsules and sealed archives are born of the same instinct: to **bear witness**. They are time machines made of boxes and locks, silent until their appointed hour arrives.

Commemorative Coins and Olympic Torches: Symbols in Motion

Not all commemorative objects are meant to be buried or sealed. Some are meant to **circulate**, to **travel**, and to **mark the passage of time in public view**. Among the most enduring examples are commemorative coins and the Olympic torch—two objects that combine symbolism, ritual, and mobility in powerful ways.

Commemorative coins have a long history, stretching back to the ancient world. In **ancient Rome**, emperors issued special coinage to mark military victories, royal births, or major public works. These coins often featured portraits, deities, or allegorical scenes, making them tools not only of economy but of **propaganda and memory**.

In the modern era, commemorative coins are typically not intended for general circulation but are minted to honor events—centennials, coronations, space missions, peace treaties. While their monetary value is usually nominal, their cultural value is rich. They serve as **pocket-sized monuments**, tokens of shared experience. For collectors, they form tangible timelines. For nations, they serve as markers of pride, identity, and unity.

The **Olympic torch**, by contrast, is ephemeral yet deeply symbolic. Introduced in the modern Games in 1936, the torch relay is a carefully choreographed passage of fire from Olympia, Greece, to the host city. It blends ancient myth with modern pageantry. The flame represents **continuity**, **peace**, and the **spirit of athletic excellence**, passed hand to hand, across borders, sometimes even across oceans and through space (as with the torch's trip aboard the International Space Station).

Though temporary, each torch is a **designed object**—crafted to reflect the identity of its moment. Torches vary in form, materials, and symbolism. The 1964 Tokyo torch evoked samurai swords; the 2012 London torch had 8,000 holes representing the 8,000 torchbearers. These objects are more than vessels of fire—they are carriers of meaning.

Like coins, they become **mementos**—collected, preserved, and displayed long after the flames have been extinguished. Together, coins and torches remind us that **commemoration can be both static and dynamic**, fixed in metal or moving through time and space.

Remembering to Be Remembered

In all their diversity—clay jars, metal coins, sealed capsules, flickering torches—these commemorative objects share a core truth: they reflect the human need to **anchor meaning in matter**. We are not content to live and vanish. We want to leave signs, markers, relics. We want the future to know we were here—and that we cared about something.

These artifacts operate on different timescales. Some speak to eternity (the Egyptian tomb), others to the next century (the school time capsule). Some are buried to be rediscovered; others are passed from hand to hand in ritual and ceremony. But each of them is a form of **storytelling through substance**. They do not rely on someone being there to explain them. They rely on their own form, context, and materiality to carry meaning.

In a world increasingly dominated by digital ephemera—disappearing messages, algorithmic feeds, cloud-based memory—these tangible commemorative objects hold a unique appeal. They remind us that memory once required **effort**, that preservation was a **craft**, and that remembrance could take **physical form**.

Perhaps, in the end, what these objects preserve is not just history, but **hope**: hope that someone will be there to open the box, hold the coin, rekindle the flame. Hope that the act of remembering will not be lost.

They are, quite literally, **time held in the hand**.

Conclusion

"We shape our tools and thereafter our tools shape us." — Marshall McLuhan

What does it mean to be human?

Over the course of this journey through *The Ultimate Collection of Cultural Artifacts*, we've walked side by side with the great inventors, the silent sculptors, the daring visionaries, and the countless unnamed artisans who shaped the world as we know it. From clay tablets baked in the Mesopotamian sun to the pixelated dreams of the digital age, we've unearthed more than just objects — we've uncovered reflections of ourselves.

Each artifact, whether a massive monument or a whisper-thin scroll, carries within it the echo of a heartbeat. It speaks of triumphs and tragedies, of prayers muttered in the dark and celebrations under stars. It tells us how people once lived — and how they hoped to be remembered.

But cultural artifacts are not simply relics of a bygone age. They are living dialogues. They remind us not only of where we've been, but also of who we are becoming. They shape our identities, our values, and our dreams. A cathedral may be made of stone, but it also holds faith. A novel may be ink on paper, but it carries entire lifetimes of emotion and thought. A painting may be static on a canvas, yet it moves generations to feel, question, and imagine.

The Layers of Human Expression

Throughout this book, we explored the raw ingenuity of early civilizations — the first wheel rolling across dusty paths, the earliest alphabets etching meaning into clay. We gazed up at towering temples and tombs carved into cliffs, created not just for function, but for transcendence. We followed the artist's brush and the poet's pen, the engineer's blueprint and the fashion designer's thread.

Each of these chapters served as a prism, refracting the infinite colors of human expression. Together, they formed a mosaic far greater than the sum of its parts. A mosaic where art bleeds into science, where religion sparks architecture, where music borrows from mathematics, and where technology dances with storytelling.

What becomes clear is this: there is no single path of progress. There is no uniform rhythm to culture. Instead, humanity advances through collisions — of ideas, disciplines, eras, and beliefs. And through those collisions, something astonishing emerges: meaning.

A Mirror and a Compass

Cultural artifacts do more than document the past — they mirror our current selves. When we look at the Antikythera Mechanism, we don't just see an ancient computer. We see our enduring desire to decode the cosmos. When we hear the strains of Beethoven or the beat of a tribal drum, we recognize emotions we still carry today. When we study Orwell's *1984*, we confront questions that remain painfully relevant.

These pieces of culture function both as mirrors — reflecting our identity — and as compasses — guiding our future. They help us make sense of the complexities we inherit and the uncertainties we face. They challenge us to remember, to empathize, and to evolve.

In times of crisis or collapse, it is often the cultural threads that people reach for first. Not just food and shelter, but language, ritual, music, memory. It is through culture that we rediscover humanity in its most essential form. And when societies rebuild, it is through culture that they rise again — brick by brick, word by word, note by note.

Preservation as a Moral Act

The preservation of cultural artifacts is not just an academic exercise. It is a moral act. To lose a language is to silence a worldview. To destroy a sculpture is to erase an entire conversation. To neglect a tradition is to sever a thread in the fabric of human diversity.

This is not to say that everything must be frozen in time. Culture is not a museum exhibit under glass — it is a river, always moving. What matters is how we hold on to its essence while allowing it to breathe and grow.

Digital archives, open-access libraries, and global heritage initiatives all offer new ways to safeguard the legacy of our species. But so does telling stories. So does teaching. So does simply asking questions — about who made something, why they made it, and what it meant to them. In that sense, every reader becomes a curator of culture. Every curious mind becomes a guardian of memory.

The Everyday Artifact

Not all artifacts are grand or famous. Many are humble, even invisible. A worn pair of shoes, a childhood photograph, a recipe passed down through generations — these too are cultural treasures. They may not sit behind velvet ropes or beneath vaulted ceilings, but they are no less powerful. They are tokens of the everyday human experience, and often, they speak with the most intimate voice.

In the future, what will be remembered? A tweet that sparked a revolution? A handmade banner from a protest? A YouTube video that taught a forgotten language? Perhaps. The digital age has expanded the very definition of "artifact," and it's up to us to decide what to carry forward.

One thing is certain: meaning doesn't always come from mass or longevity. It often comes from context, connection, and care. When we look at objects not just as things, but as vessels of human intention, we begin to understand that the culture of tomorrow is being shaped right now — in the choices we make, the stories we share, and the communities we build.

An Ongoing Conversation

This book was never meant to be a definitive catalog. It is a conversation starter — a spark. For every artifact included, countless others await discovery, interpretation, or reinvention. Culture is vast, messy, contradictory, and beautiful. It is impossible to map in its entirety. But it is always worth exploring.

As you close this book, ask yourself: What cultural artifacts do you hold dear? What songs, books, images, or inventions have shaped your life? What would you choose to preserve if you could only save ten things from today for the future?

And what will *you* leave behind?

Will it be a creation, a kindness, a protest, a performance? Will it be a family tradition or a digital footprint? Whether you build, write, care, design, or simply bear witness — you are part of this human archive. You are one more brushstroke in the great mural of civilization.

The Anthem of Humankind

To be human is to build — not just cities, but meaning.

To be human is to remember — not just facts, but feelings.

To be human is to share — not just tools, but dreams.

Our artifacts, in all their variety and fragility, are love letters to the future. They say: *We were here. We wondered. We loved. We struggled. We created.*

Let them also say: *We hoped you would listen. We hoped you would learn. And we hoped you would create, too.*

Because the story of civilization is not yet finished. The symphony has not yet reached its final note. The masterpiece is still in progress.

And now, it's your turn.

Thank you page

www.ingramcontent.com/pod-product-compliance
Lightning Source LLC
Chambersburg PA
CBHW080344170426
43194CB00014B/2678